A SOUTHERN BELLE PRIMER

Ann Hall at Grey Oaks Mansion, Vicksburg, MS. ANN HALL

A Southern Belle Primer

Or Why Princess Margaret Will Never Be a Kappa Kappa Gamma

Maryln Schwartz

DOUBLEDAY

New York London Toronto Sydney Auckland

PUBLISHED BY DOUBLEDAY
a division of Bantam Doubleday Dell Publishing Group, Inc.
666 Fifth Avenue, New York, New York 10103

DOUBLEDAY and the portrayal of an anchor with a dolphin are trademarks
of Doubleday, a division of Bantam Doubleday Dell Publishing Group, Inc.

Book design by Marysarah Quinn

Library of Congress Cataloging-in-Publication Data
Schwartz, Maryln.
    A southern belle primer, Or Why Princess Margaret will never be a
Kappa Kappa Gamma / Maryln Schwartz. — 1st ed.
      p. cm.
    1. Southern States—Social life and customs—Humor.
    2. Women—Southern States—Social life and customs—Humor.
    I. Title.   II. Title: Southern belle primer.   III. Title: Why
Princess Margaret will never be a Kappa Kappa Gamma.
    PN6231.S64S38   1991
    975'.0082—dc20   90-28415
                                  CIP

ISBN 0-385-41667-9
Printed in the United States of America
September 1991

10

CONTENTS

To Brownie Wilson—
the most quality Southern
lady I know.

Grey Oaks Mansion, Vicksburg, MS. ANN HALL.

There is no crash course that teaches you how to be a Southern belle. You can't learn the rules by reading Amy Vanderbilt. And this is one time even Ann Landers can't help. Real Southern tradition is taught at birth by doting mothers, aunts, and grandmothers and passed down from generation to generation. An outsider just doesn't have a clue.

A newcomer has been known to spend thousands of dollars entertaining her new Southern neighbors without ever realizing that serving the wrong kind of chicken salad has gotten her blackballed from the Junior League. Or that even in the 1990s, a woman will be asked to leave the St. Cecilia's Ball in Charleston if she arrives wearing a gown that shows her ankles.

Certain behavior may be perfectly acceptable in places like London, Paris, or New York, but if you break the rules in towns like Mobile, New Orleans, or Dallas, you're going to hear about it. And rest assured, true daughters of the South never forget.

It's been more than twenty-five years, but in New

Orleans they are still talking about the time presidential daughter Lynda Bird Johnson attended a Mardi Gras ball wearing *nylon* gloves.

"Her daddy was President of the United States with a protocol adviser that came with the job," a New Orleans social arbiter still complains. "You'd think someone would have told her you don't wear nylon to a formal event. Surely somewhere in that big old White House there was a pair of white *kid* gloves."

In Alabama, a royal faux pas hasn't been forgotten for almost a hundred years. It seems a grand duke of Russia once docked his yacht in the Port of Mobile when he came to this country to attend a hunting party. Crowds gathered at the dock, thrilled to catch a glimpse of such an exotic visitor. Their excitement, however, soon turned to shock. The grand duke was feverishly smoking a cigar, blowing his smoke directly into the Mobilians' faces. A local historian explains the city's newspapers saw fit to make only one observation of the entire royal visit:

"It is the impression that the grand duke is not a gentleman."

Queen and Princess with police escorts, San Antonio Fiesta.
BILLO SMITH

And in Dallas, a more recent visit by Princess Margaret of Great Britain can also still garner a few raised eyebrows.

It was a sultry afternoon in 1985 when the British princess was being feted in a chic Dallas home. A crowd of local belles gathered, excited to meet a member of the British royal family. Of course, Princess Margaret was hardly the only royalty present. There were at least six former duchesses of the Tyler Rose Festival and an ex-Queen of the Memphis Cotton Carnival. The Southern royalty all arrived on time. The British royalty was an hour late.

Not only that, but she arrived wearing pink chiffon in the middle of the afternoon (this might have been overlooked if her shoes had not been a different shade of pink). But what really caused talk was when Princess Margaret began walking around the room puffing on a cigarette. No one could believe it. She was in the living room of the president of Neiman-Marcus, for goodness' sake.

Magnolia Plantation and gardens, Charleston, SC. CHARLESTON TRIDENT CONVENTION & VISITORS BUREAU

Any good Southern belle knows that walking around with a lighted cigarette is a no-no. All over the room you could hear the Dallas ladies whispering to one another.

That woman may be the sister of the Queen of England. She may be the relative of the last Czar of Russia. She may even have a closet full of diamond tiaras.

But the Southern belles in that room knew without a doubt—that woman would *never* make a sorority at the University of Texas.

Of course there are still some people who say the Southern belle will soon be a thing of the past. That the South is becoming as homogenized as the rest of the country.

Don't believe it. You can walk into almost any

city in the United States and find a McDonald's. But you won't find a McBelle. That's because Southern women pride themselves in being unique. Sure, they live by a strict set of rules (they never wear velvet after February 14). But they interpret life with their own Southern style. Most of all, they live their fantasies. If a belle has always dreamed of being Scarlett O'Hara, when she gets married she'll walk down the aisle dressed as Scarlett (complete with twelve bridesmaids all wearing hoopskirts and picture hats). She'll even be buried as Scarlett with an extra-wide coffin so the crinolines won't look crushed.

The belle is a breed that has endured for generation after generation. That's what she's best at—enduring and surviving. She survived General Sherman's burning Atlanta, she survived the Hari Krishnas taking over the plantations in Natchez, she survived beauty shops in Memphis that no longer use hair spray.

So forget all those stories about a Southern belle being a fragile flower that wilts at the first sign of adversity. A favorite saying in the South is a true belle is a bulldozer—she's just disguised as a powder puff. She is tough, cunning, and wily. As you may recall, in *Gone With the Wind* it was the Southern *gentlemen* who fell apart. Scarlett O'Hara made a dress out of her mama's portiers (drapes to you Yankees), dug turnips, and ran a lumber company just so she could save Tara.

A Southern belle is perfectly capable of being elected President of the United States. It certainly couldn't be any tougher than getting into the Junior League in Atlanta back in the 1960s, '70s and '80s.

CHAPTER ONE

Who Are Your People?

"Remember to be very careful of who you talk about around here. Everybody in the South is kin to each other. No matter who you bring up, you're bound to be insulting somebody's aunt, uncle, or third cousin twice removed."

—ADVICE FROM A GEORGIA BELLE TO A
FRIEND WHO WAS VISITING FROM UP NORTH

What's Your Mama's Maiden Name?

Green Leaves, Natchez, MS. NATCHEZ PILGRIMAGE TOURS

When a Southern belle talks about her roots, she's not having a Clairol crisis. In the South roots mean everything: where you come from and who you are. And where you come from is always a subject for deep discussion. If you're kin to the Walkers in Tennessee, you'll be expected to explain whether that's the *cotton* Walkers or the *commerce* Walkers. Once that's settled, it's always helpful to let people know if the Walkers are on your mama's side or your daddy's side. Southerners never tire of talking about bloodlines. Everyone is questioned. No one is exempt.

Soviet leader Mikhail Gorbachev could land in

Jackson, Mississippi, and within ten minutes someone will be sure to ask: "Gorbachev? Mmm, Gorbachev? You must be from out of town. I've never heard of any Gorbachevs in Mississippi."

Once the exact hometown is settled, then you can get down to the nitty-gritty. Tom Spangler, a courtly Mississippi gentleman who is frequently called "Mr. Jackson," even narrows this to specific neighborhoods. He explains his late mother was "the last living authority on nineteenth-century bloodlines along Jackson's 'north' State Street and its intermingling."

"Of course it's not what it used to be," he says. "But you can still keep some of the old standards. I still consider the only place in Jackson to trade for groceries to be the Jitney Jungle No. 14. Ladies don't wear hats and gloves to go there anymore, but you can still find some who dress nicely. Miss Eudora Welty shops at the Jitney Jungle No. 14. I wouldn't go anywhere else." 🍂

Natchez Pilgrimage. NATCHEZ PILGRIMAGE TOURS

Only a Native Can Be Native Born

It's not merely enough to have lived in a town for a lengthy period of time. In the South, where you were born is considered your home. It doesn't matter if you moved away the day your mother checked out of the hospital. You're a native of the town where the maternity ward was located.

Not long ago a visitor to Natchez struck up a conversation with a woman in the chamber of commerce office.

"Are you from Natchez?" the visitor wanted to know.

"Oh no, honey," said the woman. "I'm from Magnolia Springs."

"Oh, are you here for the garden club pilgrimage?" the visitor inquired.

"Of course not! I've lived in Natchez for forty-three years," the woman said indignantly. "But I'm *from* Magnolia Springs."

It's the same all over the South. A newcomer in Charleston, Savannah, or Raleigh is anyone who wasn't born in Charleston, Savannah, or Raleigh. And in the *Mobile Press Register* they carefully point out in their obituaries: "She had lived in Mobile for ninety-nine years, but she was a native of Birmingham." ❧

Oral History

It is not difficult to learn about family history or local gossip in the South. Don't waste your time going to the library or even looking up old newspaper stories. Just go to any small town and ask directions to anywhere.

What you'll get is a history lesson that's incredibly detailed. That's because Southerners are incapable of saying anything as simple as "The courthouse is two streets down, the large building on the right." Instead, they give out directions that have more drama than a TV miniseries:

"Oh, you want the courthouse. That's easy. You just go to that pink house on the corner—that's Judge Green Jr.'s house. Now don't go all the way to Judge Sr.'s house or that will confuse you for sure because Judge Sr. died two years ago and the Wade Browns bought it. They're the oil-boom Browns not the grocery-store Browns. You know they have five children and they're just ruining those beautiful floors that have been in that house since Judge Sr.'s mama made her debut and had all of Atlanta at her feet. My own mama was a contemporary of his mama, although my mama didn't invite his mama to her debut ball because Judge Sr.'s mama was too fast. Runs in the family. Judge Jr. is the one who got the Sims girl pregnant and had to marry her instead of going to West Point. But it worked out fine because her daddy sent him through law school instead and now he's making a lot more money than he

would in the army. When you get to Judge Jr.'s house turn left. On the corner you'll see the Ewell home, where they had that awful murder in 1967. Some people think it's haunted. Nonsense. Old Mrs. Ewell killed that man because he was running around with her granddaughter and wouldn't marry her. The Ewells have always been hot-blooded. Right across the street is the courthouse. But I don't know why you're bothering to go there. It's closed on Wednesday afternoon!"

Of course you can't control the direction of these oral history lessons. What natives elect to tell you always refers first to what is of local interest. Anything else sometimes gets lost along the way. A man who now lives in Dallas is a native of Pine Bluff, Arkansas. He loves to tell stories of native Pine Bluff belles.

A favorite topic is the wedding of Martha Beale, "but pronounced Bell," he explains. "Our mothers were in the same grade although my mother was a year younger. . . ." The Pine Bluff native goes on and on for twenty or thirty minutes talking about "Martha Beale's first wedding, that's what everybody here remembers her for. Of course she did later go on to other things."

After another forty-five minutes you finally learn that those "other things" about Martha Beale were reported on the front pages of newspapers all over the country and Martha Beale went on to marry again and become Martha Mitchell of Washington Watergate fame. ﹖

What's in a Name?

When Southern belles want to join local committees and organizations, they rarely have to fill out application forms to tell people who they are. That's because Southern belles have names that are walking family trees. It makes it so much easier to identify everybody during sorority Rush and Junior League teas. It doesn't matter where in the South you go, because the entire South seems to be married to one another.

In some towns you can find Davis Carlyle Sotheby and her first cousin Sotheby Carlyle Davis and they are *both* leading tours for the local pilgrimage. They also have cousins in places like Little Rock or Augusta named Carlyle Sotheby Smith and Smith Carlyle Jenkins. When cousins marry, they are likely to name their daughter Carlyle Davis Carlyle.

Many Southern names have long family histories. During The War, a woman went into labor in the middle of the Battle of Vicksburg. She gave birth, hiding out in an underground cave as bullets whizzed by. The family never would forget her bravery in having that baby while the city was under siege. The child was named Siege.

A prominent Alabama family gives a girl child the name Gypsy every other generation. This all started during The War when a family lost its home to invading Union forces. There was a newborn baby in the family, and the baby's nurse looked at the infant for the first time and cried, "poor little gypsy doesn't have a home."

The use of double first names like Rebecca Ann or Jennifer Mary are also common. Double names are usually given to honor both grandmothers.

There are lots of children in the South named Rhett and Scarlett. Almost all of their families are newcomers. Margaret Mitchell made up those names to use in *Gone With the Wind* in the 1930s. New people have picked up those names. Native Southern belles, on the other hand, have real family names that go back much further.

One belle in Savannah recalls that a magazine writer from New York once interviewed her about her hometown for an article he was doing on the South.

The writer ignored the established local Southern names and asked where in the South would he have to go to find a young girl named Scarlett. He wanted to photograph her. He thought that would be a nice touch to his article.

"Well, not in Savannah," the Georgia belle said, not pleased that he was ignoring real Southern names and real Southern heritage. "And I wouldn't bother with Atlanta either. I think you're looking for someone you might find in southern Chicago." ❧

Names with a Southern History

MARTHA—The first daughter in families that are direct descendants of Thomas Jefferson are always named Martha. The second names are different to avoid confusion. One generation might be Martha Ann and the next Martha Jane.

LADY—Belles all over the South are named Lady. A South Carolina belle during the late 1800s named her daughter Lady Jane after a character in a British novel. In succeeding generations there have been Lady Janes, Lady Anns, and Lady Carolines.

FANCY and TANCY—Fancy is a name that goes back before the Civil War. A Louisiana family named their daughter that because an older child looked at her new baby sister who had bright red hair and declared, "She's not like our other baby, she's more fancy." Every other generation now has a Fancy. Tancy came along when there were twins in one generation and Tancy rhymes with Fancy.

ROSE ANN, VIOLET ANN, IRIS ANN—Doting Southern fathers consider their daughters flowers of the South, so they quite often give them floral names.

SISTER—All over Alabama and Mississippi you find girls who are called Sister. This is not her given name, but she is called this from birth. Nieces and nephews call them Aunt Sister. There are also a lot of Southern gentlemen called Brother. ❧

Newcomers

The "old-line" Southern belles like to say that there are always some newcomers who settle in a new city and instantly become a part of Old Jackson or Old Atlanta or Old Monroeville.

In New Orleans they like to point to Margot Bennett Logan, an Atlanta girl who came to New Orleans thirty-five years ago after marrying a New Orleans doctor. Margot is a real success story. She was accepted in Junior League and had daughters who made their debuts and were in New Orleans Mardi Gras courts.

"So, see," the old line will tell you. "It can be done."

That's all true. But Margot herself explains: she wasn't a native but she still had some credentials. New Orleans was definitely in her blood.

"My husband was the second cousin of my mother. My maternal grandmother was raised here just six houses down from where we live today. I also went to Sophie Newcomb College, which is in New Orleans. I came from somewhere else, but there are definitely ties." &

The Belle of Willbrook Plantation

Margaret Williams of Orangeburg, South Carolina, is descended from four governors of South Carolina and two signers of the Declaration of Independence. She has also inherited the family flair for entertaining and once put an elaborate wedding and reception together with just forty-five minutes' notice.

Margaret never neglects

Willbrook Plantation, Orangeburg, SC.

her duties as a hostess, not even when Hurricane Hugo roared through South Carolina in 1989 just as she was entertaining a group of visiting Russians.

"We were all frantic," says her daughter, Ann Platz, who lives in Atlanta. "That storm was terrible and for a few days I couldn't get a call through. My parents live on a seven-hundred-acre plantation called Willbrook. We had no idea if they'd been blown away. Finally, Daddy answered the phone and said I should not have worried. By now I should know that my mama can cope."

Ann asked where her mother was and her father explained that she could not come to the phone. They still didn't have lights, air-conditioning, or water.

"So my mother had taken the Russians across the street to my brother's swimming pool to take a bath. She handed out her best monogrammed towels and her Neiman-Marcus soap and tried to keep everything as civilized as possible."

Margaret says, "I think everyone had a good time. We charcoaled food that thawed from the freezer on the barbecue grill and since there were no lights, we ate by candlelight, which I like to do at my dinner parties anyway."

The Russians later sent a letter saying, "Your hospitality was stronger than Hugo."

Margaret says that kind of entertaining is nothing new. There are all kinds of family stories about coping. A South Carolina ancestor, Rebecca Mott, was once put out of her home by British soldiers during the Revolutionary War.

"The British let her stay in a little place in the back while they took over the main house as headquarters," says Margaret. "That made her furious and she went into action. Just so the British couldn't use her home, she burned it down. Right to the ground. That was brave. I don't know if I could have burned my home. But that's not all of the story. The British conceded she was the victor, so that night she invited the American and British officers to dinner. Her dinner invitations were coveted. Both sides accepted."

Margaret, too, is exceedingly gracious and she can get a party going in a matter of minutes.

One recent Thanksgiving, a young couple came knocking at the Williamses' plantation-house door. Margaret's husband, Marshall, is president pro tem of the South Carolina Senate and is also a notary public. In South Carolina, a notary public can marry couples.

This couple wanted a quickie marriage ceremony, but Margaret didn't think that was quite special enough.

"I decided I would throw them a wedding," she explains. "A marriage should be an occasion to remember. I just had about forty minutes to put it together. But I knew I could do it. First I had to get the bride out of the slacks she was wearing. I decided most of all, she needed a real wedding dress."

That was not an easy task on a Thanksgiving afternoon, but Margaret came up with an appropriate gown in about fifteen minutes. A close family member had been married several times and one of the early wedding dresses had been given to grandchildren to play dress-up. The dress was hunted up and fitted on the surprised but delighted bride. Margaret then started doing the young woman's hair and makeup. She sent her daughter to pick white camellias in the garden and tie them into a bouquet with the children's hair ribbons. Margaret then decreed that the bride would walk down the grand staircase.

"We got it all together in about thirty-five minutes," she says. "But then I realized something was missing. We had no music."

Margaret dashed downstairs and located some crystal bells that were scattered throughout the house. She gave one to each grandchild and told them to ring the bells as the bride descended the staircase. Margaret then had the rest of the family stand by and hum "Here Comes the Bride." As a final touch, she called the home of a nearby daughter-in-law.

"Honey, could you rush over here with some rice. We're having a wedding and all we've got to throw is grits."

Most relatives would be incredulous at such a request. The family had just had Thanksgiving dinner a few hours before and there had been no talk of a wedding. But no one ever underestimates Margaret Williams. The daughter-in-law didn't say a word. She just brought the rice.

"If I just could have had a little more time," says Margaret. "I could have come up with a wedding cake." ❧

CHAPTER TWO

Don't Put Soup in the Finger Bowls

"What is considered trash or quality in the South has nothing to do with money. Some of the best families around here haven't had money for generations. The emphasis is on breeding and manners. No amount of money can make you quality if you don't act like quality. For instance, good Southern belles don't place much importance on paying $400 to buy a pocketbook that's got some Italian designer's initials all over it. In the South, grandmother's monogrammed napkin rings are much more important than Gucci's monogrammed luggage. To think otherwise is just considered tacky. And around here, nothing is more tacky than being tacky."

—ALABAMA BELLE DISCUSSING THE
INTRICACIES OF BEING SOUTHERN

Tacky

Tacky is a word you hear so often from Southern belles, it is almost their national anthem. *Tacky* is used to comment on why some women don't make certain social circles, why some marriages are considered doomed to failure, why some new stores just aren't going to be patronized.

Asked to explain further, most belles simply say, "It's just too tacky to talk about."

But when pressed, a Tennessee woman said she remembers a Chattanooga newcomer who never did get asked to join the Junior League.

"The girls thought she was just too tacky," the woman explained.

"What specifically was so tacky?"

"Well"—the belle shrugged her shoulders and pursed her lips—"for one thing, she puts dark meat in her chicken salad." ❧

A Southern Belle's Ten Golden Rules

1. Never serve pink lemonade at your Junior League committee meetings. It has Communist overtones.

2. Always wear white when you walk down the aisle (even if it's for the third time).

3. Never wear white shoes before Easter or after Labor Day. The only exception, of course, is if you're a bride. Bridesmaids, however, must never wear white shoes. Bridesmaids' shoes should match the punch.

4. It doesn't matter if you marry a man who doesn't know the difference between a shrimp fork and a pickle fork; you can always teach him. Just make sure he can afford to buy you both.

5. Never date your sorority sister's ex-husband until at least three years after the divorce. You might need her to write your daughter a Kappa Kappa Gamma recommendation one day. Just remember it's a lot easier to find a new man than it is to get your daughter into Kappa.

6. Never marry a man whose mother and grandmother owned silver plate instead of real silver. He's not used to quality and he'll try to cheat you on the divorce settlement.

7. It's never too soon to write a thank-you note. Some belles take the notes and a pen with them to a party. In the middle of the evening they go into the ladies' room and write a thank-you describing how much they enjoyed the dinner (naming specific items). They then put the note in the mailbox as they leave. The hostess receives it first thing in the morning. Sure this is compulsive, but you're going to have to be compulsive if you want to be president of Junior League.

8. Never show your bosom before evening and never wear an ankle bracelet before anything. Girls who wear ankle bracelets usually end up twirling batons. There has never been a baton twirler who became Miss America and there's certainly never been a baton twirler in Junior League.

9. Never chew gum in public and never smoke on the street.

10. Buy low. Sell high.

Rhodes College, Memphis, TN, 1955. RHODES COLLEGE

Grandmama's Rules

Just because they like tradition doesn't mean belles can't change and modernize to fit the current times.

"My Mississippi grandmother always said only whores and children wear red shoes," says an Alabama belle. "Of course I don't abide by that in 1990, but I'll tell you this. I still cannot get used to seeing bridesmaids wearing red dresses. It's common. And now they're even wearing black dresses to walk down the aisle. Thank goodness my grandmother isn't alive to see it."

Other belles remember that their grandmothers had four good dinner china patterns and they changed the patterns every season. They also changed bedspreads summer and winter and put slipcovers on the chairs every spring. These days one good china pattern will do.

In New Orleans, a modern belle was once told by her grandmother that it is vulgar to eat potato salad. The grandmother said, "Potato salad isn't for ladies, it is something construction workers put in their lunch boxes." The modern belle eats potato salad. But she doesn't put it on the good china.

The Mayonnaise Girls vs. the Salad Dressing Girls

Good Southern belles don't put dark meat in their chicken salad and they don't put Miracle Whip on their tomato aspic. In fact, they would never have Miracle Whip in their refrigerators. They use mayonnaise—real homemade mayonnaise. If this isn't available, Hellmann's "store bought" is a good substitute (although you might add a little lemon). Belles are not so pure in other areas: they use a lot of condensed soup mix, Cool Whip, and Marshmallow Fluff. But when it comes to mayonnaise, they are unbending.

"But I love Miracle Whip," a woman who has lived in Memphis for thirty-five years told her friends over bridge.

"My dear," one of them answered. "You were born in the Midwest, and it shows." 🙟

Does Any of This Really Matter?

There are those who will tell you none of this really matters. People break the rules all the time.

One has only to look at the Duchess of York's visit to Houston in 1989 to see just how seriously this is all still taken.

Fergie arrived in November, wearing a summer dress and white shoes. Eyebrows were raised all over town. Reporters talked about those white shoes on the ten o'clock news. The shoes were still the topic of conversation the next morning on the radio talk shows.

Finally, Her Majesty's press secretary issued a statement that there were no such seasonal rules in Great Britain.

"Well, she should have realized she was in Texas," a newspaper quoted one observer as saying. "I would rather wear my crown crooked than wear white shoes after Labor Day."

The Finger Bowl

A Charleston belle explains she knows exactly when "we really had to let go of the old ways. It was in 1973. That was when all the help went to the defense plant and we had to give up our finger bowls."

This is a lament that's heard from belles all over the South. Finger bowls were once considered a must at all elegant dinner parties. But that was at a time when there were plenty of maids and butlers to help serve.

Today, grandmothers still keep their finger bowls but admit they use them for soup more often than they use them for the original purpose.

"My own grandmother would have just had a fit if she knew I considered using a finger bowl for anything other than what it was originally intended," says a Chattanooga belle. "I have her finger bowls that go back in our family for more than a hundred years. They are so pretty, I just hated keeping them in a cabinet, so I served broth in them at a luncheon. My sister was so appalled she didn't stay for the rest of the lunch. She pleaded a headache and went home. She told me later I was just plain common. That's a real put-down in my family."

A New Orleans belle says she also serves soup

in her finger bowls, but she's going to bring them out for their intended purpose at least one more time.

"I'm going to have my granddaughters over and have a formal dinner. I'm going to use the finger bowls so they will all have a chance to see what a real formal dinner is like. We can't bring back the past, but we can certainly still give some insights." 🍃

Garden party. BILLO SMITH

The Proper Way to Use a Finger Bowl

A bowl is served to each diner before dessert. It contains warm water that sometimes has rose petals or lemon peel floating in it, and is served on a plate that has a doily.

One should gently dip one's fingers into the water and then daintily wipe the fingers on the dinner napkin. After this, it is proper to pick up the finger bowl with the right hand and the doily with the left hand, setting the doily and finger bowl down to the left of the plate to be picked up by the maid or butler. When the finger bowl and doily have been removed, the remaining empty plate signifies you are ready for dessert. ❧

The Moonlight and Magnolia Crawford Twins

Ruby and Ruth Crawford are twins and a pair of Atlanta belles who were carefully taught by their mother that "there is tacky and then there is tacky tacky."

"Our mother was a great lady who laid down the law so much," says Ruby, "that we always said she should have been a judge."

They have never forgotten her lessons and they never forget they are Southern ladies. Ruby is appalled that anyone would chew gum anywhere but in the privacy of her bedroom. Ruth won't even discuss women who smoke on the street. That really is "tacky tacky."

"We believe in moonlight, magnolias, and mint juleps," says Ruth. "We believe in dressing up." The twins have dressed alike every day of their lives, right down to their mascara and eyeshadow.

"Twins should look like twins. Everything we buy, we buy for two," says Ruby. They even have twin poodles named Kandi and Kisses who wear hair ribbons the same color as the dresses Ruth and Ruby are wearing each day.

The twins say they delight in being feminine and are firm in one thing. They just don't believe a lady ever has to tell her age. "Age is immaterial," they echo. But they do admit to having taken early retirement in 1975.

But don't ever think these Southern ladies do nothing but loll under magnolia bushes all day.

"Ruth and Ruby have done more and achieved more than most Yankee men would ever think of achieving," a friend explains. "Those are the most energetic ladies I have ever seen. They are ladies in the true Southern belle fashion: they look like cream

The Moonlight and Magnolia Crawford twins with Miss Georgia, Jamie Price.

puffs and get things done like Sherman tanks. Although I don't think they'd like being compared to anything named Sherman, being from Atlanta and all."

The twins say they were children of the Depression who grew up in Temple, Georgia. As young women they moved to Atlanta, where they wanted to work and earn enough money to go to medical school.

"But it was hard times back then," says Ruby. "There was no way we could earn enough money to put both of us through medical school, so we decided to go to law school at night."

This was at a time when young women didn't leave home to go out and work, and it certainly wasn't a time when ladies were encouraged to become lawyers.

"But that's what we wanted," says Ruth. "And that's what we did."

They got jobs at an Atlanta bank and quickly became superstars. Once they got their law degrees in night school, they went for degrees in banking and accounting and received graduate certificates from the American Institute of Banking.

They were both senior trust officers at the bank when they retired.

"When we first got into banking," says Ruby, "the bank we wanted didn't hire relatives. But we said we wouldn't work anywhere unless we could work together. The bank hired us. They must have liked us. Later we were told their only regret was that we weren't quintuplets."

The twins were so active in every phase of community work that soon people were calling them "the twenty-four-hour Crawford twins." They became very active in politics, traveling all over the country to support Jimmy Carter in his bid for the presidency, taking their poodle named Celebrity with them, and created a sensation when they all dressed alike.

"Celebrity made the NBC news," says Ruth. "We all had such a wonderful time."

The twins have never married, but point out that both have had many chances.

"We live together in a wonderful Georgian house, where we entertain all the time." They insist they have never fought over what dresses they should wear each day. It just always works out.

"We believe a woman can achieve anything she wants to and she doesn't have to be masculine to do it. Look at us. Our life has been wonderful and we're still going strong," says Ruby.

When they got out of the banking business, they started their own real estate company in Atlanta, which is extremely successful.

At ten o'clock one recent evening, they were both there working late, wearing identical red dresses while Kandi and Kisses (in identical red hair ribbons) ran playfully around the office.

"We're not about to slow down," says Ruby. "Heaven can wait, we love Atlanta."

As they contemplate their lives, they say they've done exactly what they wanted, achieved everything they wanted to achieve, and haven't had to compromise one bit of their Southern upbringing.

"During all this time," Ruby says. "We have never hired anybody who chews gum." ❧

CHAPTER THREE

Learning to Sparkle

"Southern women are known for their charm. It doesn't always come naturally. It takes a lot of tap and ballet lessons, a lot of watching aunts and grandmothers, and a lot of social situations where a young belle can get a lot of practice. All Southern belles send their daughters to dancing school. This is where they first learn to sparkle. Other lessons follow. So what if a girl never pirouettes ever again after six years of dance lessons. I was a dancing snowflake at age six. My teacher said we all had to throw back our shoulders if we wanted to be successful snowflakes. If you drooped, all you could hope for is to be a puddle. My ballet slippers are gone, but I still throw back my shoulders when I enter a room. Once you've been a snowflake, you will never again settle for being a puddle."

—ALABAMA BELLE DISCUSSING THE
MERITS OF DANCING LESSONS

Tap, Ballet, and Charm

A Southern belle starts training early to be in the spotlight. She has elaborate dance recitals with costumes that would make even Bob Mackie sit up and take notice. This love of costuming sticks with her all her life. She may never have a professional dancing career, but she will always know how to dress up and project her smile just like she learned at the Rose Myrtle Fauchon School of Tap, Ballet, and Charm. If you look closely at a Southern belle's walls, there is always a framed picture of her doing the baby rhumba at the Spring-time Potpourri Dance Recital, back when she was still in preschool.

How a girl takes to this is very important. Many a Miss Mississippi at age twenty started out by being a dancing lollipop in a recital at age five. In small Southern towns, dance teachers don't teach just tap and ballet; they also teach etiquette, manners, and what some teachers like to call "charm."

"I remember when I was growing up in Marshall, Texas," says a belle. "Marshall was too small to have anyone who taught 'charm,' so in the sixth grade, every Saturday for a month or so we would all get on a bus and go to Longview, where we took charm. Then when we were finished, we'd all go to Wyatt's Cafeteria and practice what we learned."

Southern Deb Assembly, Greenwood, MS, 1971.

Debs in training: sixth graders serving as debutante pages, Greenwood, MS.

In places like Natchez, dancing school can launch a whole career in society. For more than fifty years, during the annual springtime pilgrimage, two of the city's garden clubs present a festival pageant at the city's auditorium.

Tourists from all over the world gather to watch the young people of Natchez depict what life was like in Mississippi before the Civil War. Kindergarten children dance the maypole and teenage boys dress in Confederate uniforms and dance with their mothers. The same show is repeated year after year. It never changes.

Some tourism officials have suggested that the show be modernized because, despite the dazzling antebellum gowns, the show appears to be nothing more than an elaborate dance recital.

But nothing ever changes. Children dance the maypole in exactly the same way that their grandmothers and great-grandmothers did before them. There is much competition to see which children are given what roles. All children whose families want to be a part of this must take dancing lessons. They all do because if you don't dance the maypole at age five, you're not going to be the Queen or King of the Pilgrimage later on.

Outsiders are also amazed that even in 1990, mothers can talk their high school- and college-age sons into donning costumes and dancing the waltz in front of thousands of people. Some of these young, waltzing men are sporting punk haircuts.

"It's tradition," says a Natchez belle. There are certain things boys in certain families just know they are going to do. Their mothers see to that. You know, Jewish mothers tell their sons "You can." Southern belles tell their sons "You will." ❧

How Precious of You to Ask

A Southern belle can sing your praises to the sky or slash you completely apart with the sweetest smile and the nicest-sounding words you could ever hope to hear.

No Southern lady would ever utter a word that's harsh. So you have to understand the six basic words that are the heart and soul of any belle's vocabulary.

LOVELY—"She comes from a lovely family."
"Her people are lovely."
"She has a lovely mother [grandmother, great-aunt, third cousin once removed]."

PRECIOUS—A high compliment.
"You're so precious to think of me."
"Aren't you just the most precious thing."
"Where did you get that precious dress?"

DARLIN'—Also a high compliment, to be used along with *precious* for better emphasis.
"Your daughter is darlin' and she wears the most precious clothes."
"What a precious idea. It will make the most darlin' Junior League project."
"How is that precious husband of yours? He drives the most darlin' little sports car."

CUTE—Not exactly a high compliment, but not a complete put-down either.
"Don't you look cute!" (This means you still have an outside chance of making Kappa Kappa Gamma, but you're not as solid as you would be if you looked precious or darlin'.)

SWEET—The kiss of death.

"Who's that sweet little thing in the corner. Just look at that sweet little dress she's wearing!" (You can be sure she's thinking the girl has got to be a legacy, why else would she be in the Chi O house?)

NICE—The kiss of death with the coffin sealed.

"Well, I don't know her well, but she seems perfectly nice." (She'd better think about volunteering at the hospital because she's never going to make the Junior Auxiliary.) ❧

Mother Knows Best

Southern belles take great pains to direct their children's lives. A young woman may be born into a family whose lineage will ensure that she be considered for the honor of Queen of Mardi Gras or Queen of the Pilgrimage, but it's up to Mother to see that no mistakes are made along the way.

This kind of at-home coaching has paved the way for everyone from beauty queens to concert pianists. This goes for boys as well as girls.

Rildia Bee Cliburn gave her son Van his first piano lesson when he was barely four years old. He's now fifty-five and she's still at his side.

Along with the music, she taught him Southern manners when he was growing up in Kilgore, Texas, and Shreveport, Louisiana. She's a Southern mother who told her son "You will"—and he did. He's now an international superstar but says he never would have been anything if Mother had not been there to help him every step of the way.

In return, Van Cliburn offers his mother total devotion—from publicly reciting a sonnet he wrote for her as a child to chartering a private jet to fly her to the Soviet Union.

Mikhail and Raisa Gorbachev invited Van to play at a special benefit in Moscow in 1989. Mrs. Cliburn told Van it was a big honor but they shouldn't talk

Van Cliburn and his mother, Rildia Bee Cliburn.

about it too much. The Southern belle in her just didn't want people to think they were bragging.

At ninety-four, Rildia Bee is still sitting in a chair listening to Van practice at three o'clock in the morning. The late hour would stagger most people half her age. But not this Southern belle. These are the Cliburn hours. They go to bed at dawn. At four or five in the afternoon they are just getting up. This has been their routine for years.

Rildia Bee even comes to his rehearsals. In Moscow, Van was choosing a piano from the three offered at the Moscow Conservatory of Music. The pianist played on each one. The director of the Moscow Philharmonic thought number one sounded best. Van tended to agree with him. Then a surprisingly strong voice was heard from the seemingly empty auditorium.

"Choose number two," Rildia Bee called out to her son. Never mind the rest of the experts. He listened to Mama. He chose number two.

Cliburn now lives with his mother in a baronial

mansion in Fort Worth, Texas, where a life-size portrait of his mother hangs at the foot of the grand staircase. It was a gift from Imelda Marcos.

Every year for her birthday, he entertains with a lavish black-tie party whose coveted invitations are more elaborate than most wedding invitations. For her ninety-third birthday he had the maître d' sing operatic arias to his mother. For her ninety-fourth, the gold-engraved invitations invited guests to a Viennese evening in honor "of Mother."

On her ninetieth birthday, he was so happy that his mother was enjoying such longevity that he had a preserved version of her ninetieth birthday cake made and keeps it on display on the third floor of their home. The cake is over four feet tall and features hundreds of spun-sugar flowers.

"It was so beautiful," says Van. "Mother just couldn't bear to cut it. So the baker created a preserved version and now she can go up every day and look at it."

Van says his mother was a true Southern lady and taught him manners as well as music. Even with his worldwide fame, he is still careful to say "Yes, ma'am" and "No, ma'am" because he knows she is always watching.

He attended junior high school in Kilgore, and the basketball coach remembers that Van was over six feet tall.

"He had the most incredible hands," said the coach. "He's got the hands of Moses Malone. He was also graceful and moved well. I wanted him for the team."

Van wanted to play but told the coach he would have to ask his mother.

"Mrs. Cliburn was a lovely Southern lady," says the coach. "We all thought so much of her. She couldn't have been more gracious. She appreciated me wanting Van for the team but he couldn't join. He was already known for his piano playing. She said her son's hands had been insured for a million dollars. She said he needed to keep them in good shape for the piano."

When Van donated money to the Moscow Conservatory, he gave it in his mother's name. When he gives a dinner party, he always serves her favorite meal—baked chicken, carrots, black-eyed peas, and corn bread. He also never gives a party unless she's present.

He calls her "little precious" and she just smiles as he introduces her to movie stars and heads of state who have come to hear him play.

"You're all so precious to think of us," Rildia Bee says with a queenly Southern-belle nod.

And then, just like his mother taught him back in Kilgore, Van never forgets those manners either.

"You're just all so lovely and precious," he says. "Mother and I can't thank you enough." 🍃

CHAPTER FOUR

Silver Patterns

"My dear, this is something you must always remember. Your bosom can be fake. Your smile can be fake and your hair color can be fake. But your pearls and your silver must always be real."

—SOUTH CAROLINA GRANDMOTHER
TALKING TO HER GRANDDAUGHTER

The Choosing of the Silver

Some people are born with silver spoons—Southern belles are born with silver patterns. If you don't inherit your pattern at birth, you go down to the department store and pick it out, sometimes as early as age nine or ten. This is sort of like a First Communion for Southern belles.

Southerners are quite committed to silver patterns. They look at the silver selection as closely as some others might study the horoscope. When a girl picks Grand Baroque at age eleven, she hasn't just decided how to set her table, she's charted her course in life.

Just as Aquarians are not compatible with Capricorns, Grand Baroque girls are not to marry men whose mothers have chosen Rose Point. There are far too many conflicting roses in those patterns. Their silver clashes and so will their personalities. ❧

The Twelve Patterns of the Southern Silver Zodiac

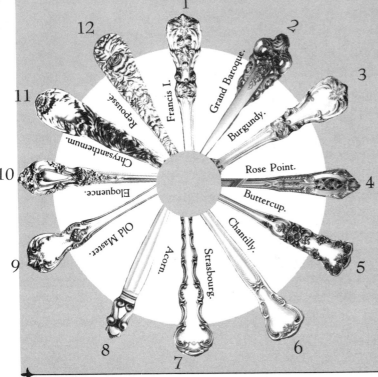

1. Francis I.
2. Grand Baroque.
3. Burgundy.
4. Rose Point.
5. Buttercup.
6. Chantilly.
7. Strasbourg.
8. Acorn.
9. Old Master.
10. Eloquence.
11. Chrysanthemum.
12. Repoussé.

1. FRANCIS I. Reed and Barton. The belle who chooses Francis I is a girl who wants it all. There are twenty-eight pieces of fruit just on the knife handle. It's showy and opulent and so is she. A Francis I girl is likely to want a husband, children, a place on the board of Junior League, and a full-time career. There is no end to what she can achieve, just as there is no end to what she can buy in the Francis I pattern. It comes with pickle forks, tomato forks, shrimp forks, lobster forks, grapefruit spoons, dessert spoons, ice cream spoons, even half olive spoons. Francis I girls are always compatible with mothers-in-law who have Grand Baroque or Burgundy. Their styles are similar.

2. GRAND BAROQUE. Wallace International.

This is Francis I with roses instead of fruit. Grand Baroque girls also have a sense of the dramatic. But they often also have a literary bent. That's why you can buy a sterling silver bookmark in the Grand Baroque pattern. Grand Baroque girls often date boys whose families have the Acorn pattern. But they don't marry them. It's just a youthful rebellion.

3. BURGUNDY. Reed and Barton.

This is Francis I without the fruit. Burgundy girls tend to be somewhat shy. They have dreams of being splashy, but they just can't let go. Louisiana girls love Burgundy. It shows up on a lot of tables during Mardi Gras. They do well with friends who have Buttercup. They are not made to feel too competitive.

4. ROSE POINT. Wallace International.

Old-fashioned girls pick this pattern. It's very popular with girls named Rose. Sentimental mothers who have chosen patterns like Old Master and Eloquence sometimes name their daughters Rose just so they can have a legacy all their own.

5. BUTTERCUP. Gorham.

Belles who choose Buttercup are always cheerful. They even choose the pattern because it's so uplifting. Buttercup girls have friends with every kind of pattern. They are usually followers rather than leaders, but they are just so upbeat it really doesn't matter.

6. CHANTILLY. Gorham.

Belles with Chantilly tend to be a bit prissy. They do best with men whose mothers also have Chantilly. Never put a Chantilly girl with a man whose mother has Francis I or Grand Baroque. They will always be upstaged. Don't let all that sweetness fool you. Chantilly girls were often fast in high school.

7. STRASBOURG. Gorham.

Strasbourg girls are traditionalists and just a bit formal. As good

Southern girls, they are entranced with anything that's festive and use their good silver almost all the time. Southern men love girls who pick Strasbourg because when Strasbourg girls bring out the good silver, they also bring out the good food. They don't mix well with boys whose mothers have Buttercup. They will both always fight for control.

8. ACORN. Georg Jensen. Beware of the Acorn girl. This pattern is lovely but foreign (it comes from Denmark). Girls who pick Acorn are rebellious. They march in parades and sometimes have been known to go to colleges in the East and drink beer straight from the can.

9. OLD MASTER. Towle. Old Master girls have spirit but don't drift too far from tradition. Because of this they are fiercely attached to their family heirlooms. One Texas belle got thirty place settings of her groom's grandmother's Old Master as a wedding gift. When she got a divorce, she took her husband to court over the Old Master and let him keep the Cadillac without a whimper.

10. ELOQUENCE. Lunt. Eloquence girls like nice things. They expect their husbands to provide. They are extremely loyal whether it's a boyfriend, a best friend, or a pet. Because of this they get along very well with more flighty girls who have Francis I or Grand Baroque.

11. CHRYSANTHEMUM. Tiffany. The Chrysanthemum girls have been known to turn up their noses at Francis I girls. The Chrysanthemums are just as flamboyant and just as demanding. They also usually have a lot more money to spend. Their husbands have to be good providers because they also insist on Tiffany crystal and Tiffany china. This is a relatively new pattern compared to some of the others. Girls with Chrysanthemum sometimes go really wild and live in avant-garde homes. But don't worry, they still cut the crusts off their tea sandwiches and their daughters always get good recommendations to Kappa, Theta, and Pi Phi.

12. REPOUSSÉ. Kirk. Repoussé is one of the oldest silver patterns. Repoussé girls often have mothers and grandmothers who also have Repoussé. One Charleston woman explains every woman in her family for three generations chose Repoussé. Then her son married a woman who didn't even have a silver pattern. The mother-in-law insisted she pick something out and had relatives fill in the place settings. When the new bride completely bypassed Repoussé by calling it "too fussy," the mother-in-law knew the marriage wouldn't last. And it didn't.

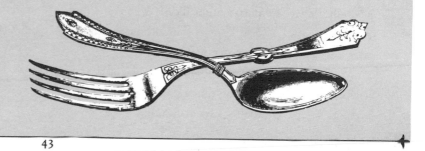

We Hid This from the Yankees

All through the South, belles will pull out silver knives and forks that are bent and have large scratches. But they are still served at the table with pride.

"My great-grandmother hid this silver by burying it in the ground during the War Between the States," an Alabama belle will tell you. Most of the time this is true, although once in a while you'll note the silversmith was a company that didn't even come into being until after World War II. Good Southern manners require that you not point this out.

Some families have magnificent silver collections with as much as twenty or thirty pieces to each place setting. They have the ice cream spoon, the ice cream fork, the shrimp fork, the lobster fork, the lemon fork, the olive fork, the half olive fork, and on and on.

"I have read my grandmother's diaries," says one Mississippi grand dame. "She used all these different silver pieces every day. She even had dinner-size silver and luncheon-size silver. No one can live like that today. They couldn't even afford the polish to keep all that silver glowing."

You can still buy silver in luncheon- and dinner-size pieces. Many choose luncheon size because it's more economical.

"I was shopping for a wedding gift for my niece,"

a Teaneck, New Jersey, woman explains. "I bought a place setting of silver and asked that the salesman be sure to give me the large dinner pieces. He didn't even pause, he just asked, 'What part of Texas do you want this sent to?'" Texas belles more than anyone else still use the big dinner pieces.

In Natchez, belles have taken to turning their family mansions into bed-and-breakfasts and taking in boarders rather than sell even one spoon from their family's silver collection. The wallpaper may be peeling and the ceiling mildewing, but the good china and silver stays in the family.

Virginia Beltzhoover Morrison was born in Natchez in the family home, which is called Green Leaves. It has been that family's home since 1849. Green Leaves is opened every year for pilgrimage and visitors can see the family's priceless china, which was hand-painted by naturalist John J. Audubon.

Once a tourist picked up a piece of the priceless china and casually tossed it in the air. The tour director was horrified and threatened to eject the man.

But the lady of the house would have none of that. She was the hostess and the tourist was a guest in her home. To smooth over his embarrassment, she began to talk as if the Beltzhoovers spent their days standing around throwing priceless china in the air. ❧

What Is Most Popular

It is difficult to say which of the top twelve silver patterns are most popular in the South. That usually differs from region to region, but most people name Francis I as the pattern most often appearing on Southern tables.

In Mobile, however, the old families are partial to the Fiddlethread pattern, which has the mark of the silversmith James Conning who crafted the silver in Mobile.

A visitor from Texas noted her family had chosen the Repoussé pattern.

"Oh really," sniffed the Mobile belle. "My great-aunt always called that *repossessed*."

A bridal consultant at Neiman-Marcus says Francis I has always been the big favorite of her customers.

"Oh, my Southern girls just love Francis I," she explains. "That's twenty-eight pieces of fruit on one knife handle. It just gives you the *shivers* to think about it." ❧

Coping

Beverly Bremer was raised to be a Southern belle who would never ever have to go to work. Then one day she found herself divorced with a small child and nothing much to fall back on except a set of Burgundy silver.

This Atlanta belle was down, but not for long.

"I suddenly began to see that silver was something I could trade for money, not just something that made up a pretty table." Then she got to work doing what all Southern women seem to be so good at. She learned to cope.

Beverly started buying and selling silver for profit.

The business in Atlanta, called Beverly Bremer Silver, became so profitable that she's now built it into one of the biggest antique (or secondhand) silver stores in the South. Brides register at her store, collectors wander in, and just plain silver buffs come to look.

Beverly sells just about any silver pattern ever made. The store is also filled with silver hollowware.

"Yes, young women still come in and pick their pattern," says Beverly. "Last week a woman came in with a ten-day-old baby. She said she was going to let the baby pick her pattern. That is the youngest I've ever seen."

She wasn't sure how the baby was supposed to be doing the picking, but the mother left happy, and that was enough for Beverly.

Not only is Beverly enthusiastic about the silver in the store, all of her employees are too. Her twenty-eight-year-old daughter, Mimi, is keeping up the tradition and works there with her. Mimi has her own favorite Southern silver story.

"A woman came in the store last year and immediately looked at a set of silver tumblers we had for sale." Mimi says even secondhand, they weren't cheap.

"The woman just sighed when she saw those tumblers. She said they were just like the ones her grandmama used to have. The grandmama would fill those tumblers with ice and Co-Cola (Southern belles always pronounce Coca-Cola this way) and she said nothing ever has tasted as good since."

Mimi says one of the saleswomen listened to this story and then slipped off into the back of the store, taking one of the silver tumblers with her. She filled the tumbler with ice and Co-Cola and handed it to the customer.

"Now, see if this doesn't taste like your grandmama's," the saleswoman said.

The customer tasted, sighed, and then smiled.

"I'll take all of them," she said.

CHAPTER FIVE

Sisters, Sisters Everywhere

"My grandmother was a Chi Omega. My mother was a Chi Omega. My two aunts were Chi Omegas, and all my cousins are Chi Omegas. If I don't get a bid to Chi O, I'll just die. I know I won't stay in Jackson, where everyone I know is a Chi O. I'll just have to move to Pittsburgh."

—MISSISSIPPI BELLE ABOUT TO GO THROUGH RUSH AT THE
UNIVERSITY OF MISSISSIPPI

"There are just some touches you find at Southern universities you won't find in the East. I remember all the sororities had their trademarks at Ole Miss back in the 1960s. I can still hear them answering the telephone at the Tri Delt house—'Delta Delta Delta, can we help ya, help ya, help ya?'"

—MAN FROM CONNECTICUT, REMEMBERING HIS DAYS AS A
STUDENT AT THE UNIVERSITY OF MISSISSIPPI IN OXFORD

Family Pressure

In true Southern tradition, mothers and grandmothers pass down their sorority affiliation with the same reverence they pass down the family jewels.

"There have been Kappa Alpha Thetas in this family for the past fifty years," a determined belle will tell her daughter. "If you come home from college a Chi Omega, you will break your grandmother's heart."

And even worse, there are always some rebellious daughters who don't want to pledge at all. At the University of Texas, a young woman whose relatives have been Kappa Alpha Thetas for decades announced she wasn't going to go through Rush Week. She was going to devote all her time to marching, demonstrating, and demanding an end to the war in Vietnam. She had no interest in sorority sings and membership teas; she was preparing for revolution.

Her horrified cousins traveled to Dallas from cities all over Texas to try to convince her she was making a big mistake.

"Just remember," they warned her. "Revolutions come and go, but Theta is forever." Finally, to please a hysterical grandmother, she pledged Kappa Alpha Theta.

Conover Hunt, Sweetheart of Sigma Chi at the University of Virginia, with escort, 1965.

"It wasn't a real satisfactory involvement," she admits. "I spent all my time protesting and was worried my more radical friends would find out I was a Theta. Of course, I didn't think they'd ever guess because I wasn't exactly sorority material when I was around them. But I hate to admit that more of those Southern manners rubbed off on me than I thought. I was at a strategy-planning session with a protest group one night and I was handed a beer. My whole life my mother told me that drinking beer straight from a can was just announcing to the world that you're common trash. Without thinking I asked for a glass. My radical friends looked at me as if I'd just announced I had leprosy. My grandmother, however, could claim a victory."

There used to be a time when a girl could always count on getting a bid to the sorority of her choice if her mother, grandmother, or other close relative had been in that sorority. She automatically became a "legacy." But today there are so many girls trying to get into Southern sororities that even ironclad legacies aren't always an insurance.

This has driven some mamas and grandmamas crazy. So they have begun taking matters into their own hands. At places like the University of Texas and the University of Mississippi, sororities begin receiving cakes, cupcakes, flowers, and an array of other gifts just as Rush Week begins.

"Just remember my daughter Jane Smith" the cupcakes might read, or an elaborately iced cake will just say the name "Jane Smith" in colorful confectionary letters.

This practice got so out of hand at the University of Mississippi that the dean of students, Judy Trott, just put an end to it, saying sororities would no longer accept these pre-Rush gifts.

"But those cakes still keep coming," says an Ole Miss Kappa Kappa Gamma. At some schools, enterprising grandmamas even fix up decorated baskets containing colorful pencils printed with their granddaughters' names to be passed out just before Rush Week. They hope each time a sorority member picks up one of those pencils, she'll remember to vote for the granddaughter when she goes through the rush parties.

. . .

Debutante with her father.

Of course, Southern mothers are shrewd women and no matter how much they've prepared their daughter to be a Kappa Kappa Gamma or a Tri Delt or anything else that has a sorority house, they also know sometimes extreme measures have to be taken. Competition is fierce.

So the more realistic mamas realize that if their daughters have no chance of becoming a Kappa at Texas during freshman Rush, there are other ways of getting there.

She just chooses a school for the daughter in some area out of state that has a Kappa chapter that isn't as choosy and hard to get into. The daughter goes to that school for a year and pledges Kappa. Then the daughter transfers to the Texas school the next year. She's already joined Kappa at the other school and Kappa is a national sorority. When she goes back to Texas, the Texas Kappas have to take her in.

Many Southern newcomers think this is silly and ridiculous and who will care in the next fifty years if someone was a Kappa or an independent or a sergeant in the army.

Southern belles never question this. They know what's important. A woman who did not grow up in the middle of a sorority family was amused some years ago to be taking part in a large conference involving top executives and high-level representatives from academia. This was a pretty powerful group—most of the people were corporation presidents and university presidents. In this high-powered crowd there were some impressive credentials being talked about.

"So I was shocked," said the woman who was not born Southern, "to listen to a speech given by the wife of a university president. She didn't talk about work or civic accomplishments, she didn't start out with her husband or family. What she wanted us to know about her was that she had been a Pi Beta Phi at the University of Texas. The woman was sixty years old and she still thought the most important thing she could say about herself was that she had been a Pi Beta Phi at the University of Texas. Isn't that outrageous?"

The woman who told the story waited for the rest of the group to laugh and agree. But these women were all born Southern.

"I'm not sure that was silly at all," said one. "You know getting a bid to Pi Beta Phi at the University of Texas is no small feat." ❧

Rush Week

Rush Week at Southern universities is a blur of ice-water teas, elaborate skit nights, and candlelight dinners where everyone is required to cry and sing sentimental sorority songs. This is all supposed to send the rushees into such a frenzy they are ready to sell the souls of their grandmothers in order to be a Kappa or a Theta or a Tri Delt or a Phi Mu. The sought-after sororities differ from school to school. The emotional pitch remains the same.

Anyone can sign up for Rush at Southern schools. The uninitiated have no idea what to expect.

First, it is essential to have letters of recommendations from past members. These letters explain how lovely a girl is, how lovely her family is, how precious her wardrobe is, and how rich her daddy is. Alums will write anything they deem necessary to get their favorite rushees into the chapter.

One Georgia Chi Omega recalls back in the seventies that someone wrote a letter giving intimate detail of the house a rushee lived in. The letter pointed out the parents loved to entertain and would always throw great Chi O parties in Atlanta. Family connections to celebrities is big plus too. If a girl could promise to get Mick Jagger to a sorority dance because he has business dealings with her father, that girl would probably get a Kappa bid. But Mick Jagger's daughter might have a hard time getting in even if her father came to visit every weekend.

Everyone who goes through Rush signs up for all parties the first day. These are ice-water teas where everyone just gets a chance to say hello for about ten minutes and then they go on to the next house. The sorority members already know who they want to concentrate on and "rush" these girls by smiling and squeezing their hands. Sororities cut down their lists as the week and the parties continue. The big night is skit night, where the sororities rewrite Broadway show tunes and dress in full costume to sing the praise of good old Phi Mu.

"I went through Rush at the university and there was this girl dressed like a scarecrow who kept squeezing my hand and singing these songs to me," says a Phi Mu alumna. "At first I didn't know if I was joining Phi Mu or joining the road show of *The Wizard of Oz*."

Although instructions explain clothes should be simple and comfortable, Southern belles go through Rush with wardrobes second only to their trousseaus.

At Southern Methodist University, where coeds tend to dress like they have an afternoon photo session for the cover of *Vogue*, the fashion show is overwhelming during Rush Week.

One girl from Chicago who was going through SMU Rush realized by the third day that she just wasn't prepared.

"I went back to the dorm," she says, "and heard all the other rushees talking. They identified everyone by the clothes they were wearing.

"There was one girl in my group who was only average-looking and went to some of the first parties. All night I heard people telling her that her Oscar was fantastic. I wondered if she had won some kind of Academy Award or if Oscar was her boyfriend. When someone told me Oscar de la Renta had designed the dress she was wearing, I knew I had a lot to learn about Southern Rush. Later I proved myself right when a sorority girl looked at my outfit and said, 'Whose is it?' I said it was mine and was insulted that she thought it looked as if it had been borrowed from someone else. As it turns out, she thought it was cute and wanted to know the name of the designer."

The final Rush Night parties bring on more tears than sitting through a showing of *Dark Victory*. If tears aren't shed, it's not a successful party. On this night sorority girls dress in evening gowns and tell their favorite pledges how life can be nothing without that Chi O pin.

"You've got to get a girl crying, get her emotional," says a Chi O alum from Ole Miss. "Sing her those sorority songs and convince her Chi O will open the doors of heaven for her. And also let her know it will get her introduced to the sharpest guys on campus." ❧

Trash or Treasure

Some universities in the South are so big, there is only a small possibility that a girl going through Rush without knowing anyone or having any recommendations will get noticed enough to pledge.

That's why in big cities, alums and sorority members visit prospective members over the summer and take them to lunch or dinner or invite them to pre-Rush parties.

These are sometimes called Trash or Treasure luncheons because alums and members get to know an upcoming rushee and report back if she is trash or treasure.

"If I had known what goes on during those sessions when they pick the girls, I never would have gone through Rush," says one girl who did get in. "We had one party that was Japanese and everyone had to take off her shoes when entering the house, which was decorated like a Japanese tea room. At the follow-up session that night, members were even discussing the cheap labels on some of the shoes and who was wearing the expensive labels."

She says she told this story to her Southern belle grandmother, who was instrumental in getting her to be a Theta.

The grandmother appeared concerned and told the granddaughter that Theta was wonderful, "but we must not be shallow and judge anyone by the kind of shoes they wear. I'm proud of you for telling me this and for telling your sorority sister this wasn't right."

Then the grandmother, being a Southern belle from head to toe, made a gift of a pair of designer pumps to every future granddaughter who went through Rush. 🍂

CHAPTER SIX

Southern Royalty

"I'm from England. I've been around royalty all my life. I was at the coronation of Queen Elizabeth II of England. The ceremony and pageantry was something to behold. But then, ten years later, I attended the coronation and some of the parties for the King and Queen of the Mobile Mardi Gras. I must say in Mobile they do things a bit more lavish. My God, they even walked down the ramp to the 'Triumphal March' from Aida. You have no idea how elaborate this all is."

—VISITOR FROM LONDON DISCUSSING
HIS IMPRESSIONS OF THE
MARDI GRAS ROYALTY IN MOBILE

Crowns

Southern belles love to wear crowns. They are obsessed with crowns. Mere tiaras will never do. Majorettes wear crowns, beauty queens wear crowns, but most of all, debutantes wear crowns. They pass them down from generation to generation along with such titles as Queen of the Mardi Gras or Princess of the Azalea Ball. One has even been called Queen of the Divine Rainbow. It really doesn't matter about the title, the important thing is to wear a crown.

In other parts of the country, when a young woman is presented to society, she wears a long white dress, is presented at a ball, and has lovely parties. But in the South, debutantes aren't just debutantes — they become queens, princesses, duchesses, or even in a few instances marchesas or maharanis.

This is no mere seasonal obligation. A Southern belle is born knowing she is going to be Southern royalty. If her mother was a Queen or a Princess or a Duchess of the Pilgrimage or the Fiesta or the Cotton Carnival, then she knows one day if she does well in dancing school, behaves herself at her grandmother's pink teas, and has a daddy who is willing to mortgage the family home to pay for her royal

robes, then she, too, will one day wear a crown and sit on a throne.

There is nothing democratic about this. Old native families control this part of Southern society. Outsiders are rarely asked. In San Antonio, Texas, a Houstonian with connections in San Antonio pointed out that his daughter had been presented at balls all over Texas. He had money and would see to it she had a magnificent court dress for the coronation of the

Queen of Fiesta. She was never asked. The father was furious to discover that an almost impoverished young woman from Houston was chosen and that she had to borrow money to buy her royal robes.

"She doesn't even live in a good neighborhood in Houston," the father of the rejected daughter complained to the committee who chose the Fiesta royalty.

"But her mother was a Queen and her grand-mother was a Queen," he was told. "This is more than *mere money*. The girl has royal blood."

And just as Princess Stephanie and Princess Caroline were trained for their duties from birth in Monaco, so are the Southern Mardi Gras and pilgrimage queens.

"Actually, I think the training is even better in the South," says a New Orleans dancing school teacher. "I don't know of any Southern Queen who behaves as trashy as some of those European princesses."

During pilgrimage week in cities all over the South, elaborate flags are flown outside certain homes. One visitor to Natchez was asked if some foreign dignitary was visiting. There were just so many flags.

"Oh no," she was told. "Those flags just mean that someone living in that house was once King or Queen of the Pilgrimage. It signifies that royalty lives inside."

Where there is a Queen or a princess or a duchess, there is always a coronation with military color guards and pages and equerries and lots of trains and scepters. Royal robes are often trimmed in ermine with elaborate designs in rhinestones, pearls, and sequins and the costs have been known to go as high as $15,000 or $20,000.

Once there's been royalty in the family, it's hard for a girl to say no when it's time for her to assume the throne. One New Orleans girl at first refused to become Queen of one of the important Mardi Gras balls. Her father put an end to her independence by insisting. "If you don't become Queen, you will be ruining everything I worked for in this city for the past thirty years." She very shortly was wearing a crown.

Even young ladies who have moved away from the South to a new and exciting life-style cannot resist the draw of becoming Southern royalty.

Jessica Albright was living in New York and in the Broadway production of *Bye Bye Birdie* when it was her year to become a lady of the court at the Mobile Mardi Gras.

She went to director Gower Champion and told him she had to take time off to be in the Mardi Gras coronation. It was a family tradition and that year her sister, Mary Jane (who also had a successful New York career), was going to be Queen. Champion released her from the show, but thought she was out of her mind.

"We had both been in show business," recalls Mary Jane today, "and actually being in the Mardi Gras court was just more show business. It was very dramatic."

Not only do the women dress up in royal costumes for these events, but so do the King and knights of the court, who wear powdered wigs and satin knickers and white stockings.

"It's a good thing there are so many parties," recalls one of the knights of the court, "because you have to get very drunk to appear like that in public."

A Duchess of Memphi

Tootie Madison Haas grew up in Little Rock, Arkansas, where she was treated from birth as a little princess. No one doubted that one day she would be royalty somewhere. She was raised in the Southern royalty tradition.

"I was born in 1949," she explained. "My mother was a true Southern belle with satin lingerie and lots of bed jackets. I grew up going to cotillions and of course dancing school." Tap, ballet, and charm came at an early age for Tootie. She was in toe shows at age three.

When she married she moved to Memphis, where her husband and his family were very much a part

Tootie Madison Haas, Duchess of Memphi, Memphis.

of society and in 1985 she was asked to be a duchess of the Memphis Cotton Carnival (now called the Great River Carnival). There are many activities and many queens of various aspects of this week, but among the most socially significant is the title of Queen or Duchess of the Crewe of Memphi. There is such a steady stream of parties during the week of the reign of the Memphi royalty that one almost never leaves the country club.

"So for that whole week, we all just moved into the Memphis Country Club. They have rooms there just for this purpose. The clothes and the costumes were spectacular. The husbands don't work during that week and there are people there to do your makeup."

She says the Queen of Memphi can spend as much as $50,000 during this week for clothes and entertaining. Duchesses don't have to go above $20,000. Tootie even won a prize that year for one of the parties' most spectacular costumes. She came as a butterfly with six feet of glittering wings strapped to her. Everything was jeweled, including her mask.

"It is a great honor to be asked to be a duchess," she explains. But in this case, it didn't ensure that she would be royalty forever. Despite the incredible wardrobe and all the clever costuming, a few years later she was out of the royal circle completely when she divorced her husband.

"And that was it," she explains.

The Little Rock princess who became a duchess and never thought she'd have to work a day in her life now puts in about sixty hours a week as director of public relations and advertising for the Peabody Hotel in Memphis.

And in true Southern-belle fashion, she says she's not only coping well, she loves it.

"I decide what to do with millions of dollars' worth of advertising," she says. "Southern belles learn to handle any situation. The training stayed with me."

Queen's Ball, San Antonio Fiesta. BILLO SMITH

Texas Royalty

Texas royalty particularly glitters and sparkles. That's because they don't stop at just being queens and princesses. Texas girls even become empresses. No court gown is too elaborate to dream up as long as the sequins and rhinestones hold out.

The most spectacular Texas coronations are the coronation of the Queen of the Fiesta in San Antonio and the coronation for the Rose Festival in Tyler. These debutantes don't just have crowns, they have jeweled and/or feathered headdresses and elaborately designed costumes. All royal court activities revolve around a theme, and every year there is a new court and a new theme. To help choose the themes there is a Royalty Chairman in Tyler and a Mistress of the Robes in San Antonio.

For the Court of Beauty in San Antonio one year, there was a Duchess of the Illusive Rainbow. For the Court of India, a deb was the Duchess of Deep Sea Divers.

In Tyler, the theme was once Journey to Imaginary Places. An Empress of the Emerald City was presented here and a Duchess of Turtle Creek, in gold from head to toe, whose theme was Eldorado.

In San Antonio, all the ladies of the court wear trains.

Carol Stollenwerk, Duchess of Dallas, Tyler Rose Festival, 1987.

Duchesses waiting to be presented, San Antonio Fiesta. BILLO SMITH

"The Queen's train can weigh as much as eighty pounds," says George Ames, a past president of the Order of the Alamo, the organization that chooses the San Antonio Queen and ladies of the court. He says the ladies of the court have to carry around only forty pounds of train.

"My wife, Annabel, was Queen of the Court of Beauty," he says. "She's tall and could handle the train. But some girls have to put wheels or rollers on the hems just so they can move."

In Tyler, they're very proud of the spectacular Rose Festival costumes.

"They are much more elaborate than in San Antonio, you know," a belle makes sure to mention.

The full court bow. JOE LAIRD/DALLAS MORNING NEWS

Of course, in San Antonio there's a difference of opinion. "Tyler is nice," a belle will say. "But theirs is nowhere near the elaborate production ours is in San Antonio."

The Texas royalty even bows differently than anywhere else. They perform what is called the full court bow. In other parts of the world, it's known as the Texas bow. These debs kneel, wrapping one leg around the other, and then bow all the way to the floor with their foreheads actually touching the floor.

"They have bow lessons for months," says a Texas belle. "But it's got to be perfect. It's not easy being royalty in Texas. But then, Texas belles never like to be like everyone else." ❧

Just Don't Show an Ankle in Charleston

While debutante events can be royal and flashy in most parts of the South, they don't go in for that kind of display in Charleston. The most exclusive social event in Charleston, the St. Cecilia Society's Ball, is still a study in decorum and quiet taste, although most people have to take someone else's word for it. Outsiders are never allowed to attend; most natives have never been. The local newspaper doesn't even write it up. Members would be horrified.

Membership is passed from father to son. The only way a woman is ever allowed to attend the ball is to be the daughter or the wife of a member. Music is sedate. Smoking is forbidden.

If the daughter of a member marries someone who isn't a member, she is no longer invited to attend. No divorced woman can attend. Some say there is still a rule that actresses are not welcome. A divorced man may attend, but if he remarries a divorced woman, he cannot attend.

"Some men wait to remarry until their daughters are past debutante age so their daughters can be presented at St. Cecilia's," explains the wife of a member.

There are no queens or princesses at this ball. The big honor is to be Bride of the Ball. This usually goes to the most recent bride, who traditionally wears her wedding gown to lead the march to the midnight supper. Couples have been known to plan their wedding dates in order to capture this honor.

The St. Cecilia Society has not let up on rules over the years. A member explains that if a woman arrives with an ankle showing, she will probably be asked to leave. If her gloves are not the proper length, she will receive a letter after the ball.

Why would anyone put up with such rules in the 1990s?

"It's just tradition," a Charleston belle explains. "And in Charleston, tradition is everything. We don't need jeweled robes and glittering crowns to know that we belong. That would be just too tacky. If you get an invitation to the St. Cecilia's Ball, that's quite enough. It's the same as a royal decree." &

CHAPTER SEVEN

Here Comes the Bride

A tape of the bride singing "Love Will Keep Us Together" was played as the guests walked into the church. Next a tape of the bride and groom talking about how they fell in love was played as an instrumental version of "Unchained Melody" could be heard in the background. Forty-five feet of greenery clipped from the yard of the bride's grandmother decorated the pews. The grandmother, Mrs. Pearl Estes, chose a powder-blue ankle-length tea dress, which she purchased at Rich's department store in Atlanta, where the bride's trousseau was also purchased. In keeping with the powder-blue and seafoam-green colors of the wedding, the bride's mother wore a seafoam-green floor-length gown which she bought at Marshall Field's department store in Chicago while visiting family members. The groom's mother, Jesse Newton, wore a seafoam tea-length dress designed and created by her sister, Olive Perkins of Montgomery, Alabama. As part of her bridal ensemble, the bride wore a gold bracelet from Tiffany & Co. that was a gift from her uncle, Aaron Sims, who now resides in New York City. The couple went on to a honeymoon at the Grand Hotel in Point Clear, Alabama, a sentimental favorite place of the bride, who celebrated her sixteenth birthday there during a family vacation.

—DESCRIPTION OF THE WEDDING FROM A SMALL-TOWN NEWSPAPER IN THE MISSISSIPPI DELTA COUNTRY

Living the Fantasy

Southern belles go all-out for their weddings. It's as if they are living a fantasy. The weddings may be small and intimate or they may be big and overflowing. But, in all cases, the bride is encouraged to express her creativity.

Personal touches are always important, and no more so than on the wedding cake. Caroline Morris of Baltimore, Maryland, says she will never forget her cousin Susie's wedding twenty-six years ago in Macon, Georgia.

"The wedding cake was the most incredible thing I had ever seen. There was a miniature staircase going down the seven different layers of the cake. On each staircase was a replica figure of someone who had been important in the lives of the bride and groom. The bride and groom were centered at the top in exact replicas of their wedding clothes. Sparklers were placed all over the cake and they were lit just before the cutting.

In small Southern towns, weddings are often the biggest social events the towns ever get to see. Small-town newspapers print everything about prominent weddings, including what the bride ate for breakfast on the big day.

In a small Tennessee town one bridal party description went like this:

The bride-to-be was feted with a kitchen shower Tuesday night at the home of her aunt, Mary Lee Robertson. One of the first gifts opened was a personalized cookie jar in the bride's wedding color of peach. Her new name was painted on the jar in the script design surrounded by flowers in a rainbow of colors. The artist was Anna Simpson, who taught the bride-to-be in the sixth grade.

The story went on to list all twenty-one people in attendance and exactly what their gifts were.

The really big fantasy weddings seem to take place in Texas. In Houston, a recent bride had eighty people in her wedding party as bridesmaids and groomsmen. It was so big, Dillard's Department Store held a special seminar just to coordinate everyone's wedding outfits. The bride kept her bridesmaids informed of the wedding progress by putting out a newsletter for several months before the big event.

But the Texas wedding that everyone is still talking about is the 1986 wedding of Danny Faulkner, Jr., of Garland, Texas, and Debbie Jordan of Phenix City, Alabama.

The groom's father, Danny Faulkner, Sr., gave the wedding so his son could have the fantasy wedding he'd always wanted. "And tonight," said the new father-in-law, "Debbie will be Cinderella."

He hired the Oklahoma Symphony to play. As the guests were escorted to their seats, the orchestra played the theme from the TV show "Dallas." The bride wore a $20,000 wedding dress supplied by the father-in-law, and as the happy couple were proclaimed man and wife, the orchestra struck up the victory song from the movie *Rocky*. 🙢

Wedding of Amy and Jamie Brenner, Brookhaven, MS.
TAYLOR CANTRELL PHOTO DESIGN

Bridesmaids

In the South, if a girl's dress matches the punch, then you know she's a bridesmaid.

Back in the 1950s, the most popular color for wedding attendants was lime green because the most popular punch of that era was lime sherbet and ginger ale.

But this is the 1990s, and the world and the flavorings have gotten a lot more sophisticated. Today a bride can choose any color of the rainbow for her wedding and she can be sure that somewhere there's going to be a sherbet to match.

But a wedding attendant's duties don't end with just getting dressed. Pledging yourself to be a bridesmaid is no simple matter in places like Charlotte, Jackson, Chattanooga, or Atlanta. There are rules and duties that never, never change.

Just getting the bridesmaids to act as a unit is somewhat like training for the Rockettes. Everything is done with precision. Southern bridesmaids must wear their hair in the exact same style when walking down the aisle and they must have it done by the exact same hairdresser. The same goes for their makeup, the color of their nails, the color of their lipstick, and the color of their shoes, which they dye to match exactly the color of their gowns.

Dyeing your shoes purple in Montgomery might turn out a different shade than dyeing your shoes purple in Macon. All bridesmaids must have their shoes dyed at the very same shoe shop. This is essential.

Then there's the girl who keeps the guest book, the girl who serves the bride's cake, the girl who

serves the groom's cake, the girl who lights the candles on the altar, the girl who helps dress the bride. These people are an honored part of the wedding party too. They also have to match the punch, as well as match the mints on the table and match the tablecloth. It is also important for the girl who cuts the bride's cake to wear the exact same shade of eyeshadow as the girl who cuts the groom's cake. If not, it could throw off the whole theme of the re-

Amy Brenner and her attendants.
TAYLOR CANTRELL PHOTO DESIGN

ception, and that would be a most upsetting way for a bride and groom to leave for their honeymoon.

Southern brides tend to have a lot of attendants. Therefore, it's often a real test of friendship to go along with the color bridesmaid dress the bride has picked, even though baby pink with hot pink highlights is your least favorite color scheme in the whole wide world. Just remember, your time will come soon enough and you can get even by picking harvest-gold dresses with rust cummerbunds when it's the current bride's time to be your bridesmaid. Then it will be your turn to look beautiful in your designer white dress while her skin turns the most awful shade of yellow from all those harvest-gold highlights.

And last but not least are the duties of the Southern bridal party. The most important being that the bridesmaids keep track of all the ribbon from pre-wedding shower presents. They then weave all these ribbons into a huge bouquet that's carried by the "substitute bride" at the wedding rehearsal.

It is a great honor to be chosen as the substitute bride. This is usually a close friend of the bride's who takes the role of the bride at the rehearsal. It's considered bad luck for the real bride to walk down the aisle at rehearsal. We hear it's done sometimes by girls in the North. But in the South, that's just tempting fate.

Flower girls. TAYLOR CANTRELL PHOTO DESIGN

The friends who keep the bridal book, cut the cake, serve the punch, and hand out the rice packets are considered an integral part of the party. They are the House Party.

"I couldn't believe in the South they think it's an honor to serve the punch," says a young woman from Vermont who was asked to be in the House Party of a friend she was in school with at Harvard University. "The wedding was in Savannah and it was quite lovely, but I hardly got to dance, I was serving the punch. In Vermont, we pay people to do that."

In big weddings, several friends are tapped for House Party duties for the same job. Bridal consultants make out computerized lists and hand them out to House Party members with exact times and exact positioning at the punch bowls and the cake.

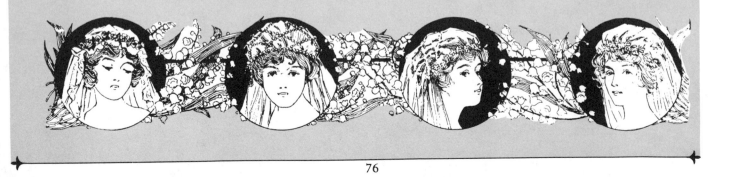

The Sip 'n' See

Southern belles know there are unwritten rules about what is proper to give as wedding gifts. Such essentials as toasters, blenders, electric knives, and microwave ovens are proper for shower gifts. Correct wedding gifts are items like china, silver, cut-glass bowls, brass candlesticks, or something antique.

"But I married someone from Cleveland," one Alabama belle remembers. "He had a perfectly lovely family but they had no idea about Southern ways. They kept sending wedding gifts like electric clocks, Tupperware, and even a tool kit. My mother had a fit because, of course, we were going to display the gifts in the dining room. Mother had tables set up, draped in white fabric. Friends could then drop by and look at the gift display."

She says her mother carefully put all the toasters and clock radios underneath the draped skirts at the gift table. When the Cleveland relatives arrived for viewing the table, their gifts were pulled out and displayed. After the Ohio contingent left, the gifts went right back under the table.

"My mother had a reputation to uphold," recalls the Birmingham woman. "We couldn't have a toaster oven sitting next to all my Francis I silver. That would have just been too tacky."

Displaying the gifts used to be something lovingly arranged by the mother, grandmother, aunt, or godmother of the bride. But today, all over the South, there are professionals who come in and arrange the gifts to show them off to their maximum advantage. It's like arranging a department store window for Christmas.

And keeping up with an old tradition, there are specific parties just to look at the gifts. A sip 'n' see is given by the bride's mother so that friends can sip wine or tea and see the presents. In some smaller towns, there is also a separate viewing of the bride's lingerie and honeymoon clothes. This is called a trousseau tea. Everything the bride plans to wear on her honeymoon is on display, including bras and panties.

There is no detail overlooked in planning a Southern belle's wedding. An Arkansas woman remembers back in the 1940s it was considered essential for the bride to arrive in a limousine at the church. Everybody does this today, but in the midst of World War II in Pine Bluff, Arkansas, this was considered the height of chic.

There was, of course, a problem. At the time, there was only one limousine in all of Pine Bluff. It was owned by the funeral home.

"But it all worked out really well," the Pine Bluff woman recalls. "The funerals were always during the day and the weddings were at night. You could have a wedding and a funeral on the same day and never really overlap."

But when it was time for this belle's wedding, her husband was in the army and couldn't get to Pine Bluff. The wedding had to be scheduled for Coffeyville, Kansas.

"Of course the first thing Mama and I did was get on a train and head for Coffeyville to make plans," says the Arkansas woman. "When we stepped off the train we took a cab to the funeral home to arrange for the limousine. The morticians were appalled. No one in Coffeyville ever thought of using the funeral parlor limousine. I hear they talked about us for years."

Today, Southern belles find it more romantic to arrive in horse-drawn carriages. One Dallas couple was so taken by Prince Charles and Princess Diana's wedding, they wanted a horse-drawn coach to take them from the church to the reception at a Dallas hotel. They had no trouble locating a coach but still had to scrap the idea. The city would not give a permit for a horse-drawn coach to get on the expressway. So the family put the newly married couple in a Rolls-Royce and had a guard dressed in costume standing at the toll booth at the entrance to the expressway, throwing in quarters for all the guests who were going on to the reception. ࿔

CHAPTER EIGHT

Life in the Big League

"It's been twenty-five years since I found out that no matter what I did, I wasn't going to be asked to join Junior League in Mobile. I just wasn't considered "old" Mobile. I won't lie to you, I was devastated. Then my sister-in-law came to visit from Wisconsin. She said they take anybody in Junior League in Wisconsin. All you had to do was ask. I never heard of that before."

—MOBILE WOMAN TALKING ABOUT JUNIOR
LEAGUE AND ITS SOCIAL SIGNIFICANCE
IN THE SOUTH

Things Aren't What They Used to Be

"You want to know the difference between the Old South and the New South," a belle from Atlanta explains. "I'll tell you the difference. This is the New South—Junior League just isn't what it used to be. They are taking in everybody now, I mean *everybody*."

For years, Junior League in places like Atlanta, Mobile, Memphis, and Charleston was an organization of women who worked day and night to help a lot of people who they would never allow in as members. That's because the League has been a longtime social tradition for Southern belles. In Mississippi, one woman says there used to be a saying: "First there's Chi O, then you get married, then there's Junior League, then you die."

Being asked to join has always been an event; it was almost like sorority Rush. Some places they sent telegrams, others engraved invitations. Grateful grandmothers would give teas to celebrate their granddaughters' being asked to join.

But despite the social significance, the League has always been an organization where belles were required to work at a charitable endeavor, just like they do at Junior Leagues in less social parts of the country.

"But there's always a special touch in the South," recalls an Atlanta Junior Leaguer. "I mean, you work really hard, so hard in fact that when I was in the League the president was always given a maid. It came with being president. I'm sure it still does."

Some older former Leaguers say they don't remember such a thing. It's just too ridiculous, it couldn't be true.

"It's just silly," said one. "I mean, just listen to how silly that sounds. I can't think of anyone who would be president of the League who didn't already have a maid."

But in 1990, that's a thing of the past. Junior League is a national organization and national headquarters says anyone wanting to join Junior League should be given membership. This has caused shock waves all through the South.

"I think it's silly for people to just think all those years of being more selective was something bad," says a Birmingham belle. "There just wasn't enough room for everybody, so you asked who you knew to join. And it's not going to change anything, you know. They'll just form some other service club that doesn't have national rules. You know, there's always room for charity work and, after all, isn't that what Junior League is all about?" ❧

Atlanta belles Penny Coppedge and Lola Battle.

Lessons Well Taught

Belles who have been active in Junior League say it's an incredible training ground for a business career.

"In places like Dallas, Houston, and Atlanta, if you are head of Junior League, you could be head of General Motors. You put forth about the same energy. These women know how to work and organize. Believe me, they could organize the Soviet Union."

Penny Coppedge and Lola Battle are two Atlanta belles who started a business from talents they helped develop in the Atlanta Junior League.

"Well, the League had a contest each year to see who could sell the most ads for the Opera Ball program," says Penny. "I learned I was really good at that. That was a thousand-dollar prize and I won each year for a long time."

"And I tell you Penny didn't let anything get in her way," says Lola. "Why, she sold an ad to the ambulance driver who was taking her daddy to the hospital."

But this was all before Lola and Penny became good friends. Penny wasn't even aware of Lola until a friend called and told her that someone named Lola Battle was selling ads like crazy. She was actually a few points ahead of Penny.

"I just went into action," says Penny. "I didn't

want to give up that thousand dollars. But I had very little time. I looked around and saw my yard people doing the lawn. I went to the head of the company and said, 'You've been doing my yard for eleven years, it's about time you took an ad for the Opera Ball.' They did and I won."

Penny's sales reputation soon began to go far beyond Junior League. Soon the owners of a new Southern magazine called *Veranda* called and wanted Penny to sell ads for them.

"I thought it sounded wonderful," she says. "But I just knew I couldn't do it alone. I wanted a partner. They said fine, now all I had to do was find the partner."

She says she was contemplating this one day when she was in church.

"I was down on my knees praying that I would find someone to help me sell ads," she says. "Then I went into another part of the church. And guess who was there—Lola. I remembered how she almost beat me selling ads for Junior League. She would be perfect. I couldn't believe it, my prayers had been answered."

They formed their own company and became whizzes at selling ads for *Veranda*.

"But we are Southern belles even when we're working," says Lola. "When we make our phone calls, we see no sense in not being comfortable. We get in the middle of the bed, put on our bed jackets, and get to work. It just makes it a lot nicer that way, don't you think." ❧

Clubs, Clubs, Clubs

Junior League is by no means the only club in the South that belles want to join. It's not even the most exclusive club. Southern belles just love to organize clubs, particularly in small towns where there just isn't much else to do.

Throughout the South, you'll find a club for almost anything with a membership that has anywhere from a one-year to a lifetime waiting list. Some lunch clubs have to be passed down from mother to daughter, other study groups get filled and then a "junior" study group is formed. Some original clubs have members in their eighties. The juniors are in their sixties.

Most clubs are built around some do-good work, although some are just plain social, like the Dress-Up Club (where the ladies dress up and go to lunch) or the Have-Fun Club (where the ladies dress up and have lunch and go to the movies). New members are asked to join; no one can just call up and request a membership.

In Memphis the La Bonheur Hospital Club is a group of women who worked long and hard to build the La Bonheur Hospital in Memphis. No one doubts their effectiveness.

But, like most Southern clubs, there have been some questions on the boundaries of good taste.

"Back when Elvis Presley was first getting real famous," says one member, "he offered to do a show for our club to raise money for the hospital. Now, he was a big star elsewhere but for some of our club members he just wasn't the type they wanted associated with their club. There was a big debate. I've never seen such arguing. But the opposition won. Elvis did not do that concert."

In Hartwell, Georgia, one belle remembers that bridge used to be a major part of the social life in the city. The individual clubs had names like the Tuesday Morning Club, the Tuesday Afternoon Club, the Wednesday Club, and so on.

"Back in the 1940s and 1950s, these were very dress-up affairs," the Hartwell belle recalls. "Even if we were just going next door, we'd wear hats and gloves. We didn't remove the hats, even when we were playing bridge."

But then a big change came over the area. A dam was being built in Hartwell and all kinds of outsiders moved in.

"They just weren't as formal about things as we were," she says. "We'd invite the newcomers to our bridge parties and our dinners and they'd come wearing the same clothes they wore around the house. It was a big difference. We got more informal too.

But she says even today those newcomers are called "the dam people." ❧

The Pollyanna Club

The Pollyanna Club of Pine Bluff, Arkansas, is still going strong despite the fact that it hasn't taken in a new member in sixty-two years.

"The Pollyannas organized in 1915 at Pine Bluff High School," says eighty-eight-year-old Helen Phillips. "In 1928, we had twenty-seven members and decided that was enough. It was about all we could handle at luncheons at each other's homes. And besides, we were getting older and didn't want some younger women coming in and showing us up. No matter how much anyone begged, we just said no."

The club took its name from the book *Pollyanna*, which was popular at the time. There are twelve members left in 1990 and they haven't missed holding a scheduled meeting in seventy-five years.

Soon after their seventy-fifth anniversary, Miss

Pollyanna Club, Pine Bluff, AK: Dot Dupree, Annetta Talbot, Helen Phillips. BECKY SHAW

Helen, Dot DuPree and Annetta Talbot were dining at the Pine Bluff Country Club and regaling the other guests with stories of their long friendship.

This was no subdued, little-old-ladies' gathering. Miss Helen drove herself up to the front door in a Lincoln Continental. Once inside, she sat down and ordered a Bloody Mary.

The Pollyannas will tell you that the first Miss America, Edith May Patterson, was a Pollyanna.

"And when that was all over," says Miss Dot, "she became an evangelist and did tent shows all over. She came to Pine Bluff with one of those shows. You've never seen such carrying-on."

"We had no choice but to go to those shows," says Miss Helen. "We had to; she was a Pollyanna."

These women have spent their whole lives in Pine Bluff. They say that girls' and women's clubs were an essential part of small Southern towns when they were growing up. The clubs shaped their lives and provided entertainment. It gave them something to do.

"You see, when we graduated high school," says Miss Annetta, "there was no question of going to work. That just wasn't done. We just waited to get married."

"And some of us were sent off to finishing school," says Miss Dot. She says they taught her how to walk into a room and out of a room. She was also instructed on how to behave at the symphony. Students were cautioned never to clap when the music ended, but to wait until the conductor turned around and took a small bow.

"And when we got all that straight they took us to St. Louis to practice what we learned. One fool girl didn't pay any attention at all. She clapped her fool head off. They never did take her back."

Miss Dot says she learned her lesson so well, she felt she was prepared for life when she returned home to Pine Bluff, where she got married and continued being a Pollyanna.

"Of course it was fifty or more years," she says, "before Pine Bluff got a symphony so I could use that clapping information." 🐌

Fallen Belles
(WELL, ALMOST)

Even belles from the loveliest of Southern families sometimes move away. They go to places like New York, Chicago, or Los Angeles and they get caught up in a world where ladies are called women and nobody wears pantyhose in the summer.

Before you know it, these belles start to like the idea of wash-and-wear hair and throwing away their eyeliner. They even open their own car doors and pretend that "red eye" refers to a late-night plane flight and not a gravy that goes with ham.

But there's something about Southern upbringing that never completely goes away. Ten telltale signs always give away a belle who is trying to "pass."

1. She calls the refrigerator the icebox.

2. Even if she's ninety, she calls her father "Daddy."

3. She would rather walk down Fifth Avenue naked than wear white shoes before Easter or after Labor Day.

4. She refers to a handbag as a pocketbook.

5. She doesn't have a couch, she has a sofa.

6. She drinks iced tea in the middle of a blizzard.

7. She will march for women's rights for twenty miles but she would die rather than walk two feet with a lighted cigarette.

8. She dyes her shoes to match her cocktail dress.

9. Her parties all have themes.

10. She has a deviled egg plate.

A Belle in Foreign Clothing

Most Southern belles are, of course, born in the South. But sometimes the stork gets off course and deposits Southern belles in Detroit, Hollywood, Washington, Las Vegas, even London and Paris.

Some obvious belles have roots that have never come even close to the Mason-Dixon line. But it doesn't make any difference. A belle is still a belle whether she's in Charleston, South Carolina, or London, England. 🍂

Court ladies, Tyler Rose Festival: "The Tin Man," "Land of Parrots," "El Dorado." TYLER AREA CHAMBER OF COMMERCE

Honorary Southern Belles

1. Elizabeth Taylor (but never Joan Collins).

2. Diana Ross (a Southern belle's dream is to be the supreme Supreme).

3. The Queen Mum of England (but not one other member of her family and that includes the late Duchess of Windsor).

4. The McGuire Sisters (their hairdos alone would get them a nomination).

5. Barbara Walters (just note how she gushes while delivering the sugar-coated poison question).

6. Eva Gabor (but never, never ZsaZsa. A Southern belle would never slap a policeman. She'd drown him with so much praise that he would never realize that he was going under for the third time).

7. Marie Antoinette (who else but a Southern belle would decide to let them eat cake).

8. Martha Stewart (those extravagant table settings are the envy of every belle from Natchez to Mobile from Memphis to St. Jo).

9. George Hamilton.

10. Willard Scott.

Paula Watson, with her
thoroughbred hunter
"Recycled," riding to the
hounds with the Hickory Creek
Hunt, Corinth, TX.

CHAPTER NINE

So Dear to Our Hearts

"I've been living in Michigan for twenty-seven years. It's not like it was when I was growing up in Monroe, Louisiana. They've never heard of a pink tea here. They've never even heard of Durkee's sauce. But sometimes in the dead of winter, I make myself a tomato sandwich and cut off all the crusts. Somehow it just helps."

—LOUISIANA BELLE TALKING ABOUT
LIVING OUTSIDE THE SOUTH

Tara Tara Tara!

There are some who believe that Tara, the home of Scarlett O'Hara, exists only in the novel *Gone With the Wind*. These people have never been south. Although there was never even a real house used in the movie (it was a studio set), all Southern belles have "the real Tara" etched in their memories. And it is almost impossible to travel to any Southern town or city without someone pointing out an antebellum home that "looks just like Tara." And usually there's a belle who resides within, dresses up like Scarlett, and gives tours.

Belles give their own Taras names like Southland, Dixieland, The Oaks, or Magnolia Point, and after the afternoon tour, the hoopskirted, modern-day Scarlett is likely to lean close and whisper to tourists, "You know this house has been in our family for generations. The story is that Margaret Mitchell once visited here and that's where she got her inspiration for Tara."

In Vicksburg, Mississippi, Rose Ann Hall delights in putting on antebellum attire and giving tours of her home, Gray Oaks.

There is even a painting of Rose Ann on the wall that friends point to and note, "Now, look at that painting. She really does look like Scarlett."

"I love to play it up," she says. "When I am

giving tours, I come down the staircase in my hoopskirts and pick out a man who is part of the tour group. I announce that he's going to be Rhett, my escort. Then I just link my arm through his and take everyone all through the house."

In nearby Natchez, there is even a California-born Scarlett.

Lonnie Riches, who is now in her forties, was just two years old when she saw *Gone With the Wind*. Ever since, she has been obsessed with living like Scarlett O'Hara. She was luckier than most. Her husband, a successful Los Angeles developer, also had Southern fantasies.

"And then one day," says Lonnie, "we went a little crazy. We bought Monmouth" (an old home in Natchez that looks like Tara). Their white-columned mansion was built in 1818 by a former Mississippi governor and general. The couple has done such an authentic restoration on the home that they have accomplished what once would have been impossible in Natchez.

They have been accepted and are considered a part of Natchez society. Their Mississippi plantation has been turned into a bed-and-breakfast and the Riches are always there during pilgrimage, dressed up like Rhett and Scarlett, greeting their guests.

"They are nice people," says one Natchez belle. "And they are lucky. It's getting so expensive to keep up these old homes that anyone who comes along and does a good job of bringing an old home back to its former glory is going to become a part of things a lot quicker than would have happened when the old families still had oil money."

In Atlanta, Betty Talmadge, wife of a former governor and senator, runs Lovejoy Plantation (an old family home she won in a bitter divorce). She rents out Lovejoy for dinners and barbecues and has named all the barnyard animals after Confederate generals. ❧

Boone Hall Plantation, Charleston, SC. CHARLESTON TRIDENT CONVENTION & VISITORS BUREAU

Southern Hair

Big hair has always been a fashion statement in the South. Teasing has not gone out of style. Hair spray sales are awesome.

"To a Southern girl," says Dallas hairdresser Karen Purvis, "getting her first can of hair spray is far more important than getting her first bra."

The Dallas hairdresser says there's a good reason for this.

"When we gave up our hoopskirts and our waist cinchers, we had to do something to keep those waists looking tiny. Big hair took the place of those big hoopskirts."

Atlanta hairdresser Carey Carter does work for L'Oréal hair products, whose base is in France.

"They (the French) refer to the Southern look as a "frosted helmet." But the Southern belles love that look. I can't talk them out of it."

He says belles love to be blondes, so they want heavy frosting. He can rarely talk a real belle into something more subtle, like highlighting.

A fellow hairdresser at the Carter–Barnes hair salon also notes that Southern belles don't go in for the wash-and-wear look.

"A Southern belle will pay $60,000 for a new convertible," says hairdresser Marc Moss, "and then she won't put down the top because it will mess up her hair."

In Houston, hairdresser Lyndon Johnson says Texas women particularly like "big" Southern hairdos.

"I think the 'T' in Texas is for *tease*," he explains. "I've teased hair so high it looks like Mount Vesuvius erupting." ❧

Chicken Salad

Jewish mothers dispense chicken soup; Southern belles dispense chicken salad. It is, of course, served with congealed Jello-O salad with a dab of mayonnaise on the top.

The basic chicken salad recipe is simple. White meat of chicken cut in dainty pieces, chopped eggs, celery, and mayonnaise. Some add minced onion, but real connoisseurs tell you that's a Yankee affectation. Southern chicken salad is served in finger sandwiches (with the crusts cut off) or stuffed in a tomato half.

It is also a staple in Southern luncheon restaurants or in Southern tea rooms.

"But Southern belles are very careful about where they eat chicken salad," says a Tennessee belle. "We all grew up knowing there were places your mama let you eat chicken salad and places your mama didn't let you eat chicken salad." ❧

Iced Tea and Deviled Egg Plates

Want to know if someone is a real Southern belle? Just look in her cupboard. If she's got an iced tea pitcher and a deviled egg plate, you can bet she's as Southern as tomato aspic. If not, she probably moved to New Orleans when she was two or three from someplace like Chicago.

Southerners don't just drink iced tea, they practically inhale it. They see no reason not to drink it when snow is on the ground. It's equally as appropriate in the middle of a heat wave.

The drink is so much a part of the South that belles find it difficult to go to other parts of the country where they can't automatically order this staple in homes and restaurants.

"I was in Syracuse, New York," recalls one Tennessee belle. "It was October and a bit nippy outside. I was with relatives and we all ordered pizza. Then I asked for iced tea. The waiter looked at me like I was crazy.

" 'It's out of season,' he said. I informed him that this was not strawberries I was talking about. Iced tea doesn't have a season. He looked kind of ill, but he made some up for me."

Iced beverages are always served at Southern tables. People from other places have always found this hard to fathom. When Bloomingdale's opened a store in Dallas, the manager of the crystal and china department had to make a special request that large beverage glasses be shipped as part of the merchandise to be sold. The New York buyers obviously did not understand just how important iced tea and iced water is in the South. And much to the horror of the local Southern belles, they didn't automatically ship iced tea spoons either.

"Up north, they just stir their iced tea with their coffee spoons," observes one belle. "It's so tacky."

The manager of the Dallas Bloomingdale's crystal department told the *Dallas Morning News* he had to get the New York buyers to come to Texas and see for themselves just how much iced tea is being consumed in the South.

Then he took one of the buyers to a restaurant called the Dixie House, where iced tea is served in thirty-two-ounce glasses and waiters keep coming around to refill them. The store manager said the buyer was incredulous.

"You mean they refill those huge glasses for free?" the buyer kept saying over and over.

Buyers who don't usually cater to the Southern market are also a bit skeptical about deviled egg plates. They just don't order them as a matter of course.

"I was in Philadelphia and asked for a deviled egg plate," says a Hattiesburg, Mississippi, belle. "The saleswoman looked at me strangely and said whatever would I use one for. I couldn't believe it. In the South, you can't get through visiting after a funeral without a deviled egg plate. You just can't put deviled eggs on regular plates, they get all tacky."

She also remembers that deviled eggs, although disguised somewhat with pickle relish, always require real mayonnaise just like any other Southern specialty.

"I'll never forget a picnic where a friend of my mother's once served us deviled eggs that didn't have any mayonnaise in them at all. It was some fancy kind of oil and mustard she'd gotten from some book. We were all appalled but too polite to say anything. She had them on a deviled egg plate just like they were the real thing. But she didn't fool anybody. If it doesn't have mayonnaise, it isn't a deviled egg."

The Vicksburg Tomato Sandwich

Most Southern customs are universally Southern. But some are unique to certain cities and they just don't mean as much anywhere else.

In Vicksburg, there is the famous Vicksburg tomato sandwich. People all over the South eat tomato sandwiches. But somehow this delicacy has more social significance in Vicksburg.

"There is a right way and a wrong way to make the Vicksburg tomato sandwich," a Mississippi belle explains. "You take a round cookie cutter and cut fresh white bread in rounds. This you spread with mayonnaise. Then you very thinly slice a tomato the exact same size as the round of bread. Carefully drain

Southern tea table. DERRO EVANS

this between paper towels so the tomato does not get runny and make the sandwich soggy. You place the tomato on the top of the mayonnaise. If you feel like being creative, you might add a pinch of garlic or, if you're very daring, even a little curry powder."

She says tomato sandwiches are always served at cocktail parties given by "old" Vicksburg. To not do it is a social faux pas.

"If you're *old* Vicksburg and you don't serve tomato sandwiches, you will be *discussed*."

Antebellum hallroom, Vicksburg, MS. VICKSBURG CONVENTION & VISITORS BUREAU

Ask Southerners what the most popular religions are in the South and they are quick to tell you—Baptist, Methodist, and football.

Southern women have a ready answer for this obsession with the gridiron. They say Southern men lost The War and they are just determined not to lose anything else ever again. Having a winning football team helps ease the memory of General Robert E. Lee's surrender.

Almost everyone in the South appears to be obsessed with the game. Even junior high games are well attended. That's because everyone knows they're watching the players that one day are going to lead Alabama and Georgia and Mississippi and all the other Southern teams to victory.

Southern football coaches are folk heroes. One

Kilgore Rangerettes, Kilgore College, Kilgore, TX.
KILGORE JUNIOR COLLEGE

Dixie Darling, University of Southern Mississippi. UNIVERSITY OF SOUTHERN MISSISSIPPI

belle remembers being in a wedding where Coach Bear Bryant of the University of Alabama was a guest.

"All the bridesmaids walked down the aisle without breaking stride," she says. "Then, when we got even with the seating row that Coach Bryant was on, we kind of stopped and sort of nodded. It was almost like bowing to royalty.

Football is also a big part of lunch and dinner conversations in the South. An Alabama belle says she doesn't recall a childhood meal without some talk of sports. When she finally visited realtives in Chicago, she was surprised to see them serve dessert and leave the table without talking about football.

"All I could think," she says, "was that the meal *couldn't* be over. We hadn't discussed football yet."

Homecoming football games in the South are legendary. Homecoming at the University of Mississippi has alums coming back year after year, still dressing up in suit and tie and still getting teary-eyed over the obligatory tailgate picnic.

Susan Johns, who now lives in Florida, says she has never missed a tailgate picnic at an Old Miss homecoming since she graduated in 1965.

"In 1967 I was nine months pregnant and traveled from Monroe, Louisiana, to Oxford for the game. I started having labor pains in the fourth quarter; the baby came two weeks early."

When she finally went back home to Monroe with her new baby, her doctor was upset with her. Why had she taken such a long car trip when she was so near her due date?

"But I reminded him it was homecoming," she says. "Then he understood." ❧

Theme Parties

Tea in Dallas. DERRO EVANS

Southern belles love things to be coordinated. Their shoes match their cocktail dresses, their tablecloths match the drapes, they even like to have their dress-up outfits match their husband's tie. Their shoes and pocketbooks always match.

"It's just keeping things in order," says one belle. "Everything just has to fit together. It makes things more comfortable."

But most of all, belles love to keep their parties coordinated. They have a theme for everything. It's something they learn from early childhood from their grandmothers, who are still fond of giving pink teas.

This is a regular tea with a polished silver tea service and tiny sandwiches that have the crusts cut off. But this tea has a theme. Everything is pink. The tablecloth is pink, the napkins are pink, the petit fours are pink, and the butter mints on the table are pink.

"The hostesses wear pink and sometimes they serve pink tea, but this isn't necessary," says a Louisiana social consultant. "Of course, the sandwiches and cakes are particularly tiny at this kind of tea. You can always tell just how fancy a tea is by how tiny the food is that is served. Anything that's big enough to fill you up is just tacky."

The Southern queen of theme parties is Houston belle Lynn Wyatt, who entertains all over the world and has never lost her Southern touch.

Mrs. Wyatt always gives her parties a theme. If it's an exotic party, she decorates the whole house in animal prints, right down to zebra-striped or leopard-spotted tablecloths. She doesn't stop with just napkins and a centerpiece. She does the whole house; any room in which the guests are going to be. When singer Placido Domingo came to dine, she named all the tables after operas. People love her Southern hospitality. Mick Jagger comes to her parties, and so does the Duchess of York.

But you don't have to be a jet-set Southern belle to make your theme parties exciting.

"Gosh no," says a Mobile belle. "I started back in junior high school when we had themes for our proms. Then for our debut balls and Mardi Gras parties. I remember one luncheon that was really spectacular. The honoree had on a dress that matched the tablecloth and the flowers, but that wasn't all. Her mother wore a blouse that matched the centerpiece, her sister wore a scarf that matched the centerpiece, her grandmother wore a hat that matched the centerpiece. It was all pink and seafoam green. These people knew how to plan. When they brought out the dessert, it was strawberry-pink cake and seafoam-green sherbet. There was hardly a thing planned for that party that didn't match, even the waiter's bow ties. It's those little touches that make things special." ❧

Southern Comforts in the North

Southern belles love the South, but they are by no means insulated. They travel the world, but are always careful to maintain their Southern ways.

"A friend from back home in South Carolina was in New York City picking out furniture," a belle says. "She did what she always does in South Carolina, she introduced herself to the salesman by saying, 'Hello, I'm Mrs. Jim Jones from Sumpter, South Carolina.' She could feel the salesman's eyebrows lifting. She just ignored that and went on buying furniture, spending a lot of money in a very short time. She knew exactly what she wanted. Then as she left, she gave the salesman a gracious smile and said, 'I'll bet no Northern lady makes up her mind that quickly.' "

There was a time in the 1940s and the 1950s when true Southern belles said they felt at home only in two places in New York—Tiffany's and the Waldorf-Astoria.

The Waldorf is still a favorite spot, mainly because they have a Junior League floor. You can stay in that part of the hotel only if you are a member of Junior League.

"It always made my husband feel better to know I'd have the protection of the League," says one belle. "I slept better knowing it too."

Other belles explain that the Waldorf always had a different set of room service china than they did in the main dining room.

"And when my mother was young," says the Texas belle, "she tells me all of her friends would take a piece of the Waldorf room service china home with them whenever they stayed there. There are women of a certain age [over seventy] all over the South who, to this day, still have their Waldorf-Astoria room service china although they will never admit where it came from."

Belles have also always felt a certain kinship with Tiffany's.

"They do have all that lovely silver," says a Charleston belle. "And the Chrysanthemum pattern has always been a Southern favorite."

Belles also like to order their wedding invitations from Tiffany's. But being Southern, they never take anything for granted.

"I have a friend," says an Atlanta belle, "who was ordering her daughter's wedding invitations from Tiffany's. She called from a small town in Florida. Before she would give the order, she asked if Tiffany's was still using Crane paper."

The salesperson told her they always used Crane paper.

"I was just checking to make sure you haven't lowered your standards since Avon bought you," the Florida belle explained. Then she quickly adds, "But Avon doesn't own them anymore. I know. I checked."

The Club

Country clubs are a second home to Southern belles. That's where they get married, that's where they make their debuts, and, their mothers hope with all their hearts, that's where their daughters will meet the men they will someday marry.

It doesn't matter what the name of the country club might be, a belle always refers to it as "The Club." There is always one club in every city that's The Club—no other identification is necessary.

In Atlanta, the club the belles talk about is the Piedmont Driving Club, a place that is notoriously discriminatory.

"Oh, please don't give people the impression that the driving club refers to golf," an Atlanta belle explains. "It was named for when the members used to drive in horse and carriages. And it's really changing today, I mean, it really is. They are just inviting *all kinds* of people to join now. I promise you, they really are."

The Atlanta woman says belles just feel at home at The Club. They love to have luncheons there and play bridge and, of course, plan their daughter's debuts.

"You know they don't like any business to be conducted at The Club. They get all upset. It's supposed to be just social. I remember one day we were there planning our daughter's debut and while we were waiting for some of the others to arrive, we started writing down in our notebooks what we needed.

"Well, they saw us with those notebooks and had a fit. They said we were doing business. They put us in a back room and made us pretend we were playing bridge. They are very strict at The Club." ❧

Another kind of club: the old Ladies' Lounge, Peabody Hotel, Memphis.

Anticommunism

Glasnost and *perestroika* have been a dilemma in the South. Old-time Southern belles built a good part of their lives around being anti-Communist. Mothers did not allow their daughters to trick-or-treat for UNICEF because this United Nations children's fund gave money to "Communist nations." One South Carolina belle did not bat an eyelash when her granddaughter had a baby six months after the wedding, but when the same granddaughter sent out UNICEF Christmas cards one year, the grandmother sent her a stern letter that hinted at dropping her from the will.

"We were so anti-Communist in Montgomery," one belle recalls, "that I'm sure no one would even serve borscht at the country club. It would just be too suspect."

But now the world has changed and Southern belles are changing too. Communists are actually being entertained in old Southern homes. The entertainments are even being written up in the society columns.

When Atlanta was courting other countries to vote for Atlanta to be the site of the 1996 Olympic Games, delegations from Communist countries were treated royally. It was suddenly very "in" to entertain them.

"We had these men from Bulgaria we were entertaining," says an Atlanta belle. "We decided to take them to a football game. It was the University of Georgia playing the University of Florida. I mean, this is a really big game. There is lots of partying going on all during it."

The belle says she and her husband were sitting in a box with the Bulgarians, who had no idea what was going on.

"I mean, I thought even Communists knew about football, but they didn't. They just looked amazed. I told them to just think of it as the world's largest cocktail party."

She says in the box next to them were some young, blond Southern belles who were flirting with the Bulgarian men.

"And you know how Southern belles flirt. They just went on and on. At halftime they introduced themselves. I said, 'You are going to have to talk slower. These men are from Bulgaria.'"

She says the blond belles just smiled even broader.

"Well, how do you do," one of them answered. "We're from Valdosta." ❧

Saving the Old Family Home

The women of the South have a grand sense of survival. And there is no better example of this than in Natchez. It's what got these Mississippi belles through the bitter war that pitted family against family, neighbor against neighbor, and sister against sister.

No, not the Civil War. This was the War Between the Garden Clubs.

"It was just awful," recalls one Natchez belle. "The town was torn in two. Best friends barely spoke."

But the women of Natchez have come together again, making peace amid the azaleas and magnolias.

Grey Oaks, Vicksburg, MS. ANN HALL

Once more they are united in a common cause—a passion to protect their land and their history, both threatened by an economy gone bad.

Scarlett O'Hara lived on turnips during her struggle to save Tara. Today's women of Natchez let busloads of tourists troop through their ancestral mansions. And even though several of the estates have been bought away from local residents and inhabited by Hare Krishnas, the women of Natchez are unruffled. They endured when the Union Army occupied their antebellum plantations in 1863, they'll endure while the Krishnas occupy them in the 1990s.

"We survived before," they tell you in their soft Southern inflections. "We'll survive again."

Spring Pilgrimage is a fifty-year tradition in this river city, just like it is in cities all over the South. For one month, thirty Natchez antebellum homes are opened for touring. Twenty-two are sponsored by the Pilgrimage Garden Club and seven by the Natchez Garden Club (one is shown by the Daughters of the American Revolution). Tourism is the biggest

industry as well as being a key event in the Natchez social structure.

Pilgrimage is considered so important in Natchez that founder Katherine Grafton Miller has that distinction inscribed on her tombstone: "Founder of the Natchez Pilgrimage."

Back in 1932, when the event began, there was just one garden club. Then, in 1937, a fight over how the pilgrimage money was to be distributed divided the club. The women who went through the separation say it was like the Civil War all over again.

For years, separate pilgrimages were held and each club presented separate kings and queens. But now Natchez can no longer afford a feud. The old money from cotton, land, and oil is no longer flowing. If the women wanted to save the town, they had to get together on the pilgrimage. And many of them have turned their homes into bed-and-breakfasts or opened them for the tours. A house on spring tour can make as much as $12,000. It's the only way for many to save the old family home. But no one would dream of combining the royalty. That's too steeped in tradition. Each garden club still presents its own King and Queen and each reigns for a two-week period.

Actor George Hamilton was once welcomed in Natchez. Now he's considered a traitor. He owned two historic plantations on the outskirts of the city, then moved and sold the property to a group of Hare Krishnas. The Krishna group later bought Gloucester Plantation, one of the most historic houses in Natchez. It is now being billed as a home where the Old South meets the ancient East.

"I just think of Gloucester as being occupied by outsiders now," says one garden club member. "But one day it will come back. I just know it will come back." &

Southern belles always think of themselves as girls. They may be ninety years old, but they still talk about having "the girls" over for bridge.

And when a Southern belle is particularly well thought of and has reached a certain age, she is no longer referred to as Mrs. Smith or Mrs. Brown, she becomes "Miss Clara" or "Miss Lucinda."

Dean Faulkner Wells says this was very much a custom when she was growing up in Oxford, Mississippi. And her grandmother, "Miss Maude," was a Southern belle everyone could take a lesson from.

"Every afternoon," her granddaughter recalls, "Miss Maude [mother of the writer William Faulkner] would come in the house and take a bath at about four.

"Then she'd powder herself and put on a fresh dress and her jewelry. No lady wore jewelry before four in the afternoon. After that she'd go sit on the

Barbara Buckley, Miss Texas U.S.A. 1980, dressed as "The Yellow Rose of Texas." GUYREX

gallery, fanning herself, and watch everyone go by on South Lamar Street.

"If they were people she thought were worth speaking to, she would nod to them. If not, she'd go on fanning as if those people just didn't exist."

CHAPTER TEN

Beauty Pageants

"It can take several years to train right to make it all the way to the Miss America Pageant. That's because there's so much competition, you've got to work day and night and enter everything in sight just for the practice. Getting to be Miss Texas is like getting your Ph.D. in beauty pageants."

—TEXAS BEAUTY CONTESTANT TALKING
ABOUT GOING FOR THE BIG TITLE

Karen Wallace, Miss West Texas. GUYREX

Kara Keyes, Miss Baytown, Texas. GUYREX

I Just Want to Be Miss Mississippi

Southern belles are good at winning beauty pageants. That's because they pay a lot of attention to their appearance and they train to be beauty queens the way some people go after being President of the United States. In fact, there are some who say that if Michael Dukakis had trained like a Southern beauty contestant, he'd be President today.

Before a girl becomes Miss Mississippi or Miss Texas, she may have entered as many as twenty previous pageants. No detail is too small in this training. It takes a lot of work to be natural and unassuming. But there's a lot of help along the way. Former Miss America contestants have formed businesses all over the South that just help train girls to be beauty queens.

There are even families who are pageant sponsors who will let these belles move into the sponsor homes for months at a time in order to prepare the girls for a big pageant. Each day, these sponsors watch the morning news shows and read the newspaper with their charges. They teach the contestants to discuss world events, the way a proper beauty contestant should. This ensures that the contestants will have an answer to all questions, but nothing too controversial.

Deborah Morales of Texas: tap-dancing baby beauty pageant winner.

"I believe the youth of today is the adult of tomorrow" is always a safe statement to make.

In Dallas, a woman once made a business out of taking young teenagers to the Miss America Pageant each year. It was presented like a grand tour of Europe.

She explained she was taken to Atlantic City to see the pageant when she was twelve years old. She had her picture taken standing on the Miss America ramp. It had a profound effect on her life.

For years she offered a package deal—plane tickets to Philadelphia, then bus tickets to Atlantic City, then tickets to the pageant and hotel accommodations and food. She would chaperone.

Her business boomed for ten years before she became ill and had to quit.

"Mothers loved to send their daughters with me on the trip. The mothers loved to go too. It was so educational. Just being near all that good posture was worth the trip." ❧

The Super Suit

Miss Texas U.S.A. Pageant, 1990. GUYREX

Ada Doggett of Arlington, Texas, invented what she called the Super Suit. It changed forever the bathing suit competition at the Miss America Pageant.

"I just had a basic form," she says, "and made it to build up what was best about a girl and play down what wasn't. Putting on that suit could automatically take off ten pounds just by having it fitted right."

Contestants from all over the country came to Ada to have their suits fitted. And every year the bathing suit winners had on one of Ada's suits.

But this Texas lady is famous for still another addition to beauty pageant lore. She's the person who thought of spraying the contestants' fannies with glue so the bathing suits will stay in place as they compete in the pageant. ૪ৄ

The Talent

Southern belles know how to pull together a talent competition even when they have no talent. They've learned that what really matters is putting on a good show.

For years, these girls put on satin gowns and diamond watches and read the *Gone With the Wind* scene where Scarlett promises, "I'll never be hungry again." And of course, Southern belles have always created a sensation with their fire baton routines.

But belles are quick to note when a trend has gone by. Alas, there hasn't been a serious fire baton

Miss Mississippi. Miss Mississippi Pageant

twirler in the Miss America Pageant for years. Belles have to keep up with the times if they want to keep those beauty titles coming. And now they know it's time to come up with something completely new. In the eighties, a belle roller-skated to "Amazing Grace." When she didn't even get in the top ten, the Southern girls knew it was time to become more high-tech. Be prepared for some really groundbreaking talent in the future. ♧

Southern Belle Miss America Talents for the 1990s

1. Programming a VCR (while wearing a dress she made herself).

2. FAXing right there onstage in Atlantic City to some exotic city like Tokyo (She'll show her versatility by memorizing all those extra foreign area codes. In the background, music will be playing that she picked out herself).

3. Microwaving pudding, chocolate and vanilla swirled together, while giving a speech about world togetherness.

CHAPTER ELEVEN

The War

"I never heard about anything called the Civil War until I went to Maine one summer with my mother. In Alabama, my family and my teachers always called it the War Between the States. And that was only when they were being polite."

—ALABAMA BELLE TALKING
ABOUT THE WAR

It's Like It Was Yesterday

n Alabama, belles call it the War Between the States; in Mississippi, they talk about the War of Northern Aggression, and in Charleston, South Carolina, there are belles who refer to it simply as The Late Unpleasantness.

Whatever it's called, the Civil War is still a serious subject in the South. In Vicksburg, many people still refuse to celebrate the Fourth of July. Vicksburg fell to Union forces on July 4, 1863. People say the memories are too fresh.

Roberta Alexander, Vicksburg National Military Park. VICKSBURG CONVENTION & VISITORS BUREAU

All around Vicksburg you can see reminders of The War. There is even a Battlefield Mall.

At a bed-and-breakfast called the Balfour House, owner and Vicksburg belle Terry Weinberger explains that a Christmas ball was being held at this very same Balfour House in 1863 when a stranger came running through the front door and announced that the Union forces had landed in Mississippi. The ball was

Vicksburg Siege Reenactment. VICKSBURG CONVENTION & VISITORS BUREAU

stopped and the men, already in Confederate uniforms, left immediately to defend their city.

"I recreate the ball every year," says Terry. "We do it complete with Confederate uniforms and ball gowns. But now we do it for tour groups."

But this belle, like many others in Vicksburg, is quick to point out that The War didn't just cause a schism between the North and the South. It's also caused some hard feelings between Vicksburg and nearby Natchez.

"In Natchez, they gave in to save the city," says a Vicksburg belle. "They invited the Yankee soldiers into their homes, entertained them, and gave them no resistance. As a result, Natchez was not destroyed and only one person was killed. In Vicksburg we fought, the city was destroyed. The loss of life was devastating."

The Vicksburg belle takes great pleasure in pointing out what she considers Natchez's short-comings.

"They like to tell you the first Christmas tree in Mississippi was just north of Natchez. Well, that was right. It was ninety miles north of Natchez, right here on Depot Street in Vicksburg."

A highlight of any visit to Vicksburg is a visit to the Civil War battlefield, where tour guides like seventy-seven-year-old Roberta Alexander explain that what she's telling you is family history.

"Well, I certainly wouldn't call it the Civil War," says Roberta. "There was nothing civil about it. I call it the War of Northern Aggression. We were just farmers. We didn't know those people."

When Roberta gives her tour in the heat of the summer, she carries a ruffled pink parasol to ward off the sun in the sultry heat.

"My grandfather fought in the siege of Vicksburg," she says. "He was just nineteen years old. His two brothers died at Shiloh." One of the landmarks

Balfour House Ball, Vicksburg, MS. VICKSBURG CONVENTION & VISITORS BUREAU

she points out is a massive monument erected by the state of Illinois, with the names of all 36,312 Illinois soldiers who fought in the battle of Vicksburg. The battle lasted forty-seven days.

The monument has forty-seven steps leading up to the enclosed memorial building modeled after the Pantheon in Rome.

"It just chafes me that they put forty-seven steps there," she says. "We don't need to be reminded how long the battle was."

There are no Civil War homes to visit in Atlanta. The city was burned to the ground. As a result, there are such active Civil War buffs in Atlanta that Civil War reenactors have been known to show up in uniform at Atlanta funerals.

"I remember one such funeral not long ago," says one Georgia belle. "They had four or five of those reenactors dressed in Confederate uniforms and they hadn't shaved for a day or so, as if they were really on a battlefield. They didn't come up to the grave like the real mourners but lurked in the background off in the distance. I swear it was so real I know some people who weren't sure if there were actors or ghosts out there." ☙

CHAPTER TWELVE

The Final Journey

"My mother never said anything so indelicate as 'dead' or 'death.' Not even when my uncle died after a long illness did she utter the 'D' word. She just called and informed me that my uncle had finally found relief.

"If you didn't know Southern belles, you'd probably think my uncle had just gotten rid of his indigestion, instead of having passed on from a massive heart attack."

—A VIRGINIA BELLE TALKING ABOUT
DEATH IN THE SOUTH

The Dearly Departed

No one really dies in the South. They go to their eternal rest, they pass on, they depart this life. Southern belles never have to actually say the word *death* or *die*. It's just too tacky.

But funerals are a different matter altogether. They are always on a Southern belle's mind. That's because her mama and grandmother have taught her to always be prepared.

"My mama has been after me all my life to make sure I have at least one good black dress for every season," says a Jackson belle. "That's so if some kin dies in Tupelo or Hattiesburg or Greenville, I can be there in a matter of hours always looking my best. I've finally got that part of my wardrobe complete. My mama is so happy."

She says her mama goes even further than this. She keeps at least three casseroles in the freezer at all times.

"So if someone passes on unexpectedly, she's got enough turkey tetrazzini to cover any event."

Cemeteries are not to be taken lightly in the South. The old ones, of course, are the best ones. But spaces are getting taken up rapidly. As a result, getting into a good cemetery is about as difficult as getting into a good country club. And just like at the good clubs, it helps to have references and it helps to have family connections.

Funeral food: fried chicken, iced tea, and deviled eggs.
DERRO EVANS

A Mississippi belle says her family is so obsessed with having the right final resting place that they have plots in good cemeteries all over the South.

"When I was living in Oxford," she explains, "a burial plot came up right near William Faulkner. I thought that was just too good to pass up. Of course, I bought it on the spot." In Dallas, some plots in Hillcrest Cemetery face a posh North Dallas shopping center. There are always requests from belles who stipulate they want to be buried facing Neiman-Marcus.

Most families have had plots in the best cemeteries for years. But every once in a while, financial setbacks or second marriages make it necessary to sell one of them. That's when a funeral director can start making discreet phone calls.

"Good news," a Houston belle was told recently. "I think I can get you something nice in Glenwood [the cemetery where Howard Hughes is buried]."

What to Wear

Belles are always concerned about how they look. It certainly doesn't change when they take their final journey. Texas women particularly like to be put to rest in their favorite ball gown; some Mississippi women are partial to fancy peignoir sets. In Richmond and Charleston, it would be tacky not to be wearing something suitable for church. Some families have stopped speaking to each other when a Virginia relative wants Grandmother to be buried in daytime clothes and a Mississippi granddaughter will hear of nothing short of the pink lace peignoir.

One New Orleans belle grew up collecting a hope chest, as Southern belles always used to do. When she was a teenager, her godmother even embroidered her wedding nightgown and robe. But the Louisiana belle had never married when she died at seventy-nine. She was buried in the wedding nightgown and peignoir. &

Ya'll Drop by the House

After any funeral in the South, it's just expected that everyone is going to "drop by the house afterward. Don't ya'll forget."

Of course there's food galore. Just because someone has passed on doesn't mean hostess duties can be shunned. Everyone comes and looks forward to Aunt Fanny's banana pudding or Cousin Jesse's honeyed ham with "Co-cola" gravy.

Of course Aunt Fanny and Cousin Jesse have been in their own final resting places for years, but no one else ever gets credit for the recipe. It may be fifty years later and several new generations of belles who are making that dish, but it just doesn't matter.

And while today there are a lot of new kinds of deli and pasta trays, there are certain dishes that always appear at a Southern funeral. If not, it's just not considered a Southern funeral. ❧

Top Ten Burial Casseroles
(AND OTHER ACCOMPANIMENTS)

1. Green bean casserole with cream of mushroom soup, Velveeta, and canned fried onion rings.

2. Grits casserole with grits, butter, eggs, and garlic Velveeta.

3. Chicken casserole with rice, cream of chicken soup, and Velveeta.

4. Broccoli casserole with broccoli, rice, cream of mushroom soup and Velveeta.

5. Bing cherry mold with black cherry Jell-O, bing cherries, shredded pineapple, pecans, and Co-Cola.

6. Frozen congealed fruit salad with strawberry Jell-O, sour cream, whipped cream, miniature marshmallows, and fruit cocktail (always served with a dollop of mayonnaise).

7. Deviled eggs.

8. Baked ham with Co-Cola gravy.

9. Lemon pound cake.

10. Pineapple upside down cake.

And So It Continues....

These are the 1990s and there are a lot of changes in the New South. But old-line Southern belles don't consider this a threat at all. Sure, girls from Virginia, whose grandmamas never allowed business to be discussed when the table was set with the good silver, are now joining the Marines. And young women from perfectly lovely families in Kentucky are living in places like North Dakota and using paper napkins at dinner parties.

The real Southern belle, however, knows how to adapt.

Seventy-year-old Margaret Williams, who entertained the Russians in the middle of Hurricane Hugo in South Carolina, certainly never had to go out and find a job. She concentrates on civic and philanthropic endeavors. She sets her table with Francis I and still gives the best parties around.

Her daughter, Ann Platz, however, says she's definitely a career woman. She has her own design firm in Atlanta with eighteen designers working for her. She's considered savvy and successful.

"But, yes, I'm still a Southern belle," she explains. "At my firm we're the real designing women. But it's all women. I could never hire a man to work beneath me. It's just against everything I've ever been taught." She also notes she has kept up the family tradition in silver. She is the second generation to have Francis I.

Her daughter, Margo Cloer, is twenty-one and is also living in Atlanta. Margo, too, says she is a part of the New South and feels free to become anything she wishes—in or out of the South. She has no Southern belle misgivings about women flying to the moon, starting their own businesses, or even becoming admirals in the Navy. Margo definitely plans to work.

But that doesn't mean she doesn't consider herself a belle with all the old traditions. She, too, says she would never hire a man to work for her. And when she was recently recovering from an appendectomy, she found it comforting to keep a silver ice bucket next to her bed, filled with ice.

"And of course," she says in her soft Atlanta drawl, "you can be sure the silver tongs were Francis I." &